NORMAN ROCKWELL

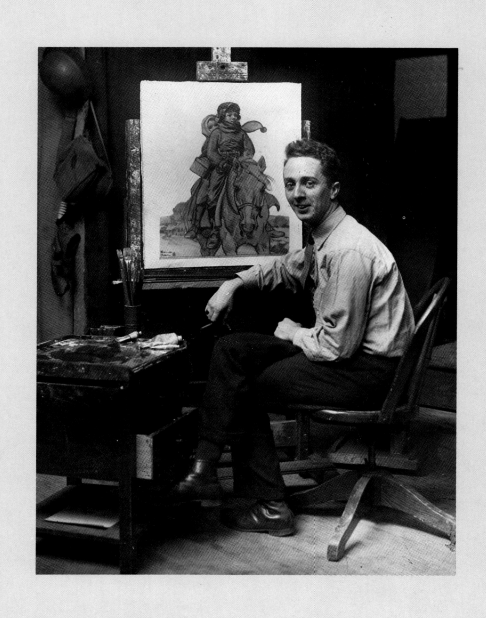

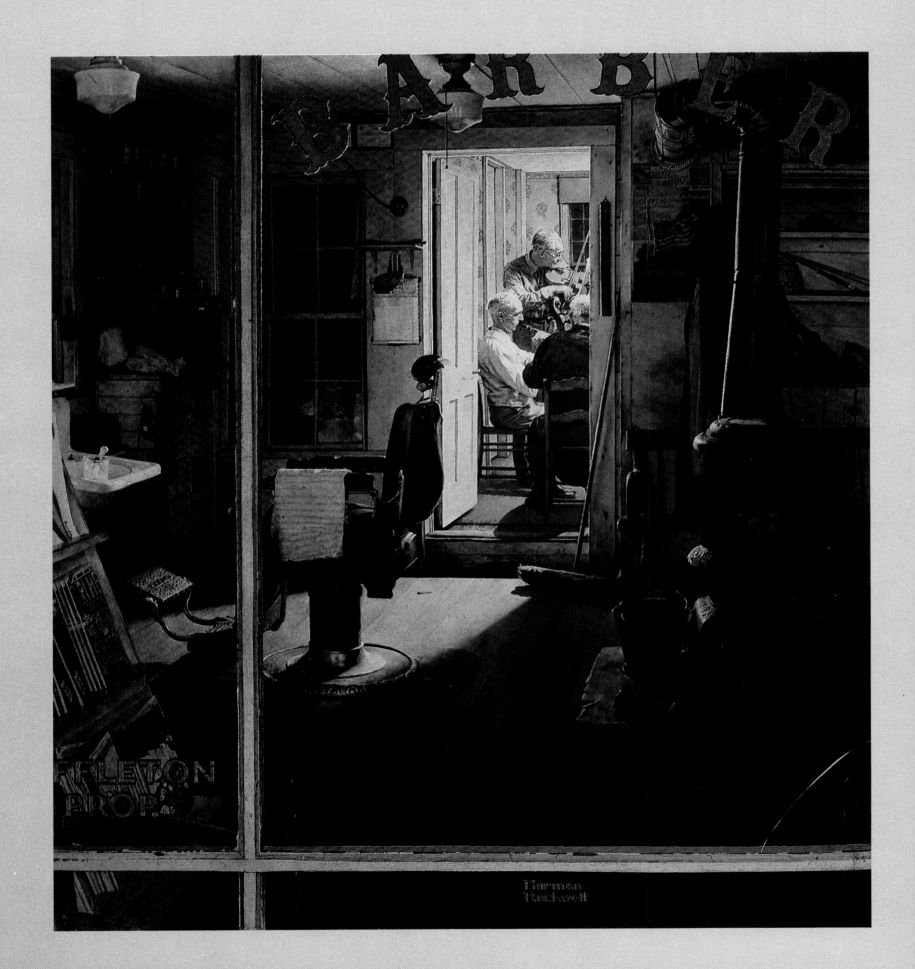

NORMAN ROCKWELL

SHERRY MARKER

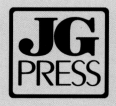

JG PRESS

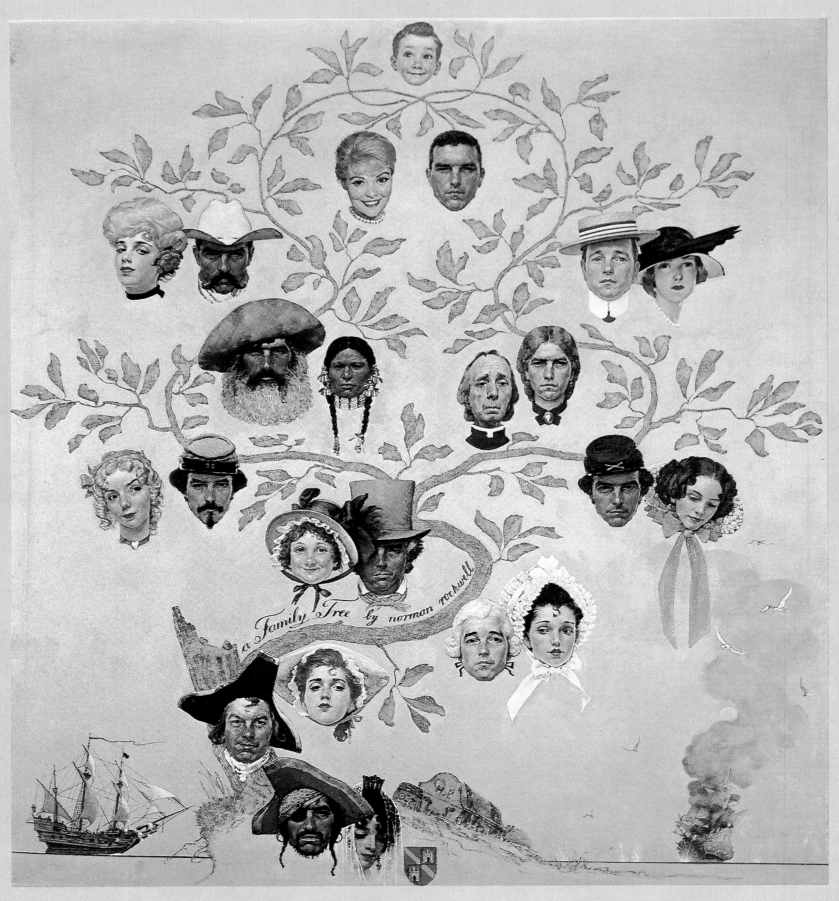

Published by World Publications Group, Inc.
455 Somerset Avenue
North Dighton, MA 02764
www.wrldpub.com

ISBN 1-57215-382-2

Printed and bound in China by Leefung-Asco Printers Trading Ltd
1 2 3 4 5   06 05 03 02

Page 1: One of the earliest photographs of Rockwell as a
professional illustrator.

Page 2: *Shuffleton's Barber Shop,* an original oil painting for a *Post*
cover, 29 April 1950.

Above: In the *Post* cover, A *Family Tree* (24 October 1959),
Rockwell paid tribute to Howard Pyle, who was famous for his
pirate illustrations, by putting Pyle's initials on the treasure chest.

Contents

Introduction 6

Human Interest 20

People and Places 40

History and Holidays 68

Portraits and Social Issues 88

List of Color Plates 112

INTRODUCTION

One of Norman Rockwell's earliest memories from his boyhood in turn-of-the-century Mamaroneck, New York, was of his father reading aloud from Charles Dickens' *David Copperfield*. As his mother sewed and his brother Jarvis bent over his homework, Norman tried to sketch the characters Dickens described. There was Mr. Micawber, "a stoutish middle-aged person . . . with no more hair on his head than there is on an egg, and with a very extensive face." Over and over, young Norman would try to capture that "extensive face." Years later, Rockwell recalled how "I'd draw Mr. Micawber's head, smudge it, erase it, and start over." At the time, the Rockwell family could not have known that the career of twentieth-century America's foremost illustrator had begun.

In 1899, as a boy of five, Rockwell sketched Admiral Dewey's flagship steaming into New York harbor after the Spanish-American War; seven decades later, in 1969, he painted the first landing on the moon for *Look* magazine. In between those years, Rockwell painted virtually all aspects of contemporary American life. His countless illustrations appeared in almost every major twentieth-century magazine – on *Saturday Evening Post* covers from 1916 to 1963, in *Boys' Life*, *Look*, and others – as well as in advertisements and books like *Tom Sawyer* and *Huckleberry Finn*. Rockwell brought his images of America into homes coast to coast; in turn, Rockwell's America reflected the way that millions of Americans fancied themselves and their country. In sixty years as a professional illustrator, he captured the embarrassments and exhilarations of childhood, the awkwardness and bliss of courtship, the exasperations and affections of family life – as well as moments of national pride and concern. Although blacks and other minorities were largely absent from Rockwell's work, his myriad depictions of white middle-class American life earned him the nickname "the American Dickens" by the time of his death in 1978.

Norman Rockwell was born in New York City in 1894, and returned there to study art as a high school student. But his boyhood – and much of his vision of America – was shaped by growing up in Mamaroneck, New York, where his family moved when Norman was nine. Significantly, Rockwell's strongest memories of his first years in New York City were trolley excursions *out* of the city into what was then the open countryside of the Bronx. Even today, Mamaroneck has broad tree-lined streets, but when the Rockwells moved there in 1903, it was more rural than suburban. Rockwell always remembered how glad he had been to leave what he called "the cold world of the city." In Mamaroneck Norman read Horatio Alger and Rover Boy stories, played baseball, dug holes to China in the backyard and enjoyed the pleasures of an all-American boyhood – despite the embarrassments of being skinny and pigeon-toed. "I looked," Rockwell recalled in his 1960 autobiography, "like a bean pole without the beans."

Although Norman Rockwell often said that the Rockwells were "distinguished by their lack of distinction," there had been money in his father's family – a family which Rockwell characterized as "substantial, well to do, character and fortunes founded on three generations of wealth." There were childhood visits to Norman's grandmother in her elegant house, and Rockwell's parents hoped that eccentric Auntie Paddock might leave them her fortune. Instead, the fortune went to buy Bibles for prisoners at Sing Sing, all except for a meager $100 legacy to Norman's older brother Jarvis. Norman's father continued to work in the New York City textile firm of George Wood, Sons and Company, where he had worked his way up from office boy to office manager – a respectable, but by no means outstanding position. All of this was particularly painful for Norman's mother, whose general unhappiness cast a long shadow over Norman's boyhood.

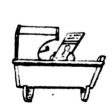
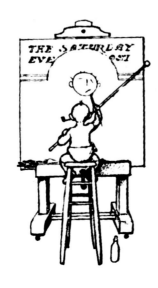
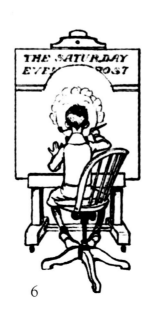
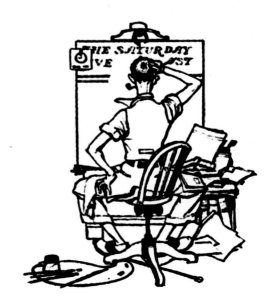

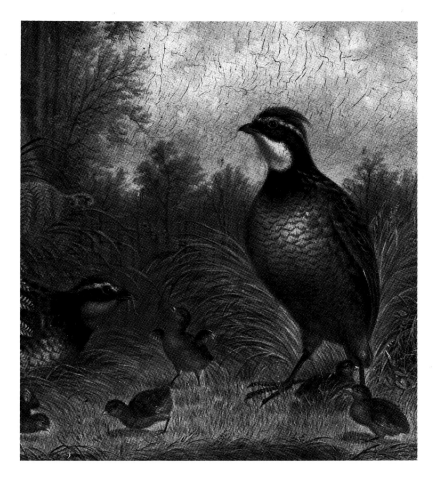

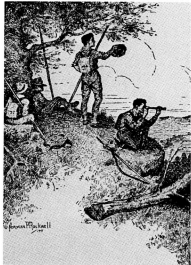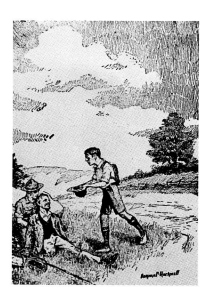

Left: A painting of quails by Rockwell's grandfather, Howard Hill.

Above and right: A few Rockwell drawings for Boy Scout hiking and camping manuals (1913-14).

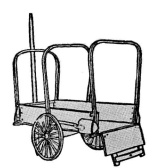

Nancy Hill Rockwell was one of twelve children of an unsuccessful portrait and landscape painter, Howard Hill, who emigrated to America shortly after the Civil War. As a child in England, Hill had sung a solo at Buckingham Palace for Queen Victoria, and nothing in his later life quite lived up to the glory of that moment. Hill eked out a living painting sentimental scenes, animal portraits, and – when all else failed – houses. Matters were not helped by his drinking problem, and Rockwell's mother always looked down on her father and identified strongly with her mother's family, the Percevels. Norman himself was named Norman Percevel in honor of Sir Norman Percevel who, according to family legend, had prevented Guy Fawkes's escape in his attempt to blow up the House of Lords in 1605; as a young man, Norman dropped the "Percevel" which had earned him taunts as a "sissy" in school.

Early in her marriage Norman's mother took to bed, complaining of vague ailments; she remained an "invalid" until her

death, years later at 85. Often she would call young Norman to her bedroom and say: "Norman Percevel, you must always honor and love your mother. She needs you." However, his mother's ailments distanced her from Norman. She was almost as remote a figure as his father, whom Norman remembered as having treated him and his brother as "sons who have grown up and been away for a long time." One of the few interests Rockwell and his father shared was sketching; Norman seems to have inherited his artistic talent from both sides of the family.

Still, the man who would grow up to be America's most beloved illustrator of family togetherness once admitted that he remembered very little of his parents. Some might suspect that he chose to forget much of life in Mamaroneck. The chill of family relations made home life almost as cold as the New York City Norman had been so glad to leave. "I paint life," Rockwell often remarked, "as I would like it to be." Rockwell's nostalgic paintings of family life portrayed the world in which he wished

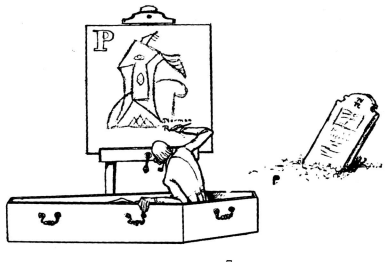

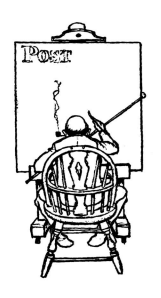

Left: "Norman Rockwell from the Cradle to the Grave" reflects the artist's long and productive years working for the *Post*, 1916 to 1963.

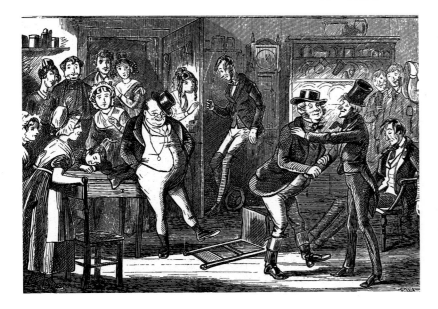

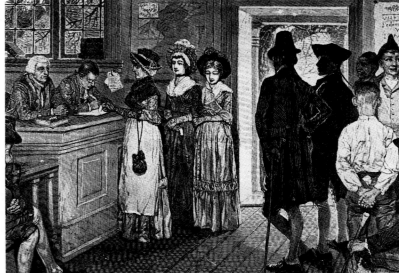

he had grown up, not the one he had known.

At an early age, Norman discovered that the one thing which gave him real pleasure at home, sketching, could also win him acclaim at school, where he was an otherwise indifferent student. When it was time to decorate the blackboard for Christmas or Thanksgiving, teachers often asked Norman to draw holiday scenes, and even the other children, who taunted his bean-pole ungainliness, admired his drawings. By the time he was a ninth-grader, Rockwell was taking the trolley into New York City twice a week to study art at the Chase School; a year later, at 16, he quit high school altogether and began to study art full-time at the National Academy of Design. The Rockwells never had an excess of money, and Norman worked at a number of jobs to earn his tuition: teaching sketching (one of his early pupils was Ethel Barrymore), delivering mail, and even tutoring other youngsters in French (a language he had never studied).

At the National Academy, Norman began his studies tentatively; he found sketching plaster casts of classical statues tedious at best. After two months, he was promoted to the life-drawing class where, he modestly recalled, "It was the first time I'd ever seen a lady up close in such decolletage." Before long, Rockwell found that the boredom of the repetitive exercises at the National Academy outweighed the pleasures of the lady models' decolletage, and he transferred to the Art Students League. There, his serious studies began in earnest with George Bridgeman and Thomas Fogarty. Bridgeman was a superb draftsman, drilling his students in the intricacies of anatomy; he reminded them that it took 11 muscles to move the little finger. Fogarty, on the other hand, urged his students to "step over the frame and live in the picture." Rockwell learned from both teachers, and prided himself on his attention to detail, as well as his ability to make a picture come alive by "stepping over the frame" and living in the picture.

The Art Students League was founded by one of America's best-known illustrators, Howard Pyle, and artists, such as Winslow Homer and Charles Dana Gibson, had studied there. Rockwell entered the school at what would prove to be the end of a golden age of illustration: Howard Pyle, and the great painter of the West, Frederic Remington, died during Rockwell's student days. Magazines were using more photographs instead of illustrations; moreover, rising production costs were limiting book illustrations, the field in which artists – like Howard Pyle, N.C. Wyeth, and A.B. Frost, illustrator of *Uncle Remus*, and John Tenniel, illustrator of *Alice in Wonderland* – had made their reputations. Along with such legendary artists as the illustrators of Dickens – H.K. Browne, known as "Phiz," and George Cruickshank – these men and their historically detailed and accurate paintings inspired young Rockwell, who in turn, never wavered from wanting to become an illustrator himself.

Fortunately for Rockwell, the advent of the four-color printing process in the 1920s gave illustrators a new lease on life. Full-page color illustrations for articles and stories rapidly became a feature item in many magazines like the *Post, McCalls*, and *Colliers*. Much of Rockwell's best work was an attempt to convey, as his teacher Thomas Fogarty put it, "an author's words in paint." Nor did Rockwell ever consider illustrators inferior to "serious" artists. As he was fond of saying: "If I had a choice between an original Rembrandt and a good Howard Pyle, I would take Howard Pyle every time." In his 1959 *Post* cover *A Family Tree*, Rockwell included a tribute to Pyle, who was famous for his depictions of pirates: Pyle's initials appear on a pirate's treasure chest.

By 1912, when Rockwell was only 18, he was already beginning to earn money for his drawings. His first published works appeared in C.H. Claudy's *Tell-Me-Why Stories about Mother Nature* (for which he made $150 for 12 black-and-white illustrations) and Gabrielle Jackson's *Maid of Middies' Haven*. Only a year later, Rockwell was publishing steadily in *Boys' Life*, for which he did 200 illustrations in two years, in additon to holding down the job of art editor at this magazine. By 1915 he could afford to leave his cramped studio in New York (located above a house of prostitution, which Rockwell was too naive to notice) and rent a larger studio in New Rochelle, New York.

New Rochelle was something of an artists' colony in the 1920s and 1930s. Perhaps the best known New Rochelle artist then (until Rockwell's own fame grew) was the illustrator

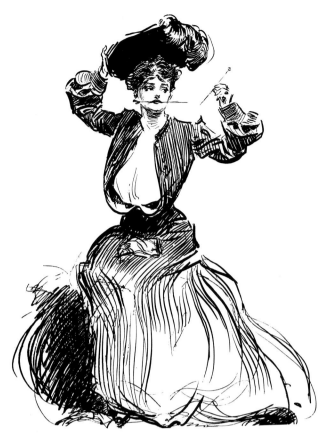

Above: Charles Dana Gibson's "Gibson Girl" was the feminine ideal in the early twentieth century.

Opposite left: A woodcut by H. K. Browne of a scene from Dickens' *The Pickwick Papers*.

Opposite right: "Woman Suffrage," a pen-and-ink drawing by Howard Pyle.

Below: *Post* cover, 20 June 1936, by J. C. Leyendecker.

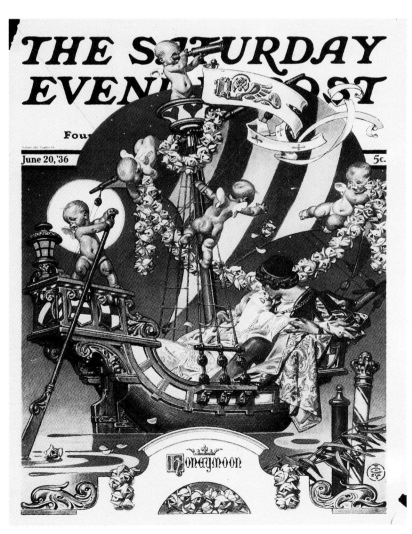

J.C. Leyendecker, whose reclusive and eccentric ways interferred with his work for the *Post* and other magazines. Rockwell spent his first few years in New Rochelle living in a boarding house. Although privacy was minimal, the range of "characters" in the boarding house more than made up for any inconvenience. As Rockwell pointed out, "I don't think there is any place in America where you can see more of human character, or the lack of it, than in a boarding house." Over the years, many of the boarding house characters gave Rockwell ideas for story and cover illustrations.

By 1915, Rockwell's career was progressing incredibly well for one so young, and he was looking beyond *Boy's Life, Saint Nicholas, The Youth's Companion* and the other childrens' magazines to which he was selling illustrations. Already, Rockwell had his sights set on doing a cover for America's most popular magazine, *The Saturday Evening Post*. Yet, for months, Rockwell held back from getting together a portfolio to show George Horace Lorimer, the dictatorial editor of the *Post*. Not for the last time, Rockwell was almost paralysed with fear and self-doubt – what if Mr. Lorimer found his work too unsophisticated? In desperation Rockwell did a series of paintings in the manner of Charles Dana Gibson: sophisticated men and women in evening clothes. When he showed them to a close friend and fellow artist Clyde Forsythe, Forsythe spelled out his verdict: "C-R-U-D."

Rockwell was crushed. But he took Forsythe's advice to forget imitating another artist, and instead to show examples of his own best style. With five paintings in a carrying case, which Rockwell later remembered as resembling a baby's coffin, the young artist nervously presented himself at the main office of the *Post* in Philadelphia. To his astonishment, two drawings were accepted on the spot, and the other three were approved for future use; for each, Rockwell collected the then lavish fee of $75. One painting, published in 1916, showed two tough boys in baseball outfits jeering at a boy in his Sunday best, who was unwillingly pushing a baby carriage. *Boy with Carriage* was the first of Rockwell's 321 *Saturday Evening Post* covers to appear over the next 47 years. From the 1920s to the 1960s, although Rockwell did an enormous amount of work that was *not* for the *Post*, the *Post* and Norman Rockwell became synonymous for millions of Americans.

For the first 20 years of his career, Rockwell always painted *every* detail from live models – and that didn't just mean using people. For example, once when Rockwell needed a duck for an illustration, he had a local butcher bring a live duck to his studio. When the duck waddled around the studio, the butcher assured Rockwell that the bird would feel no pain if its feet were tacked to the floor. That's just what Rockwell did to get his accurate drawing of the duck! Beginning in the late 1930s, Rockwell relied increasingly on photographs, which enormously simplified working with ducks, horses, children, and outdoor settings like the swimming hole in *Summer Picture*.

Rockwell's working methods were methodical. First of course, he had to come up with an idea for illustrating either a

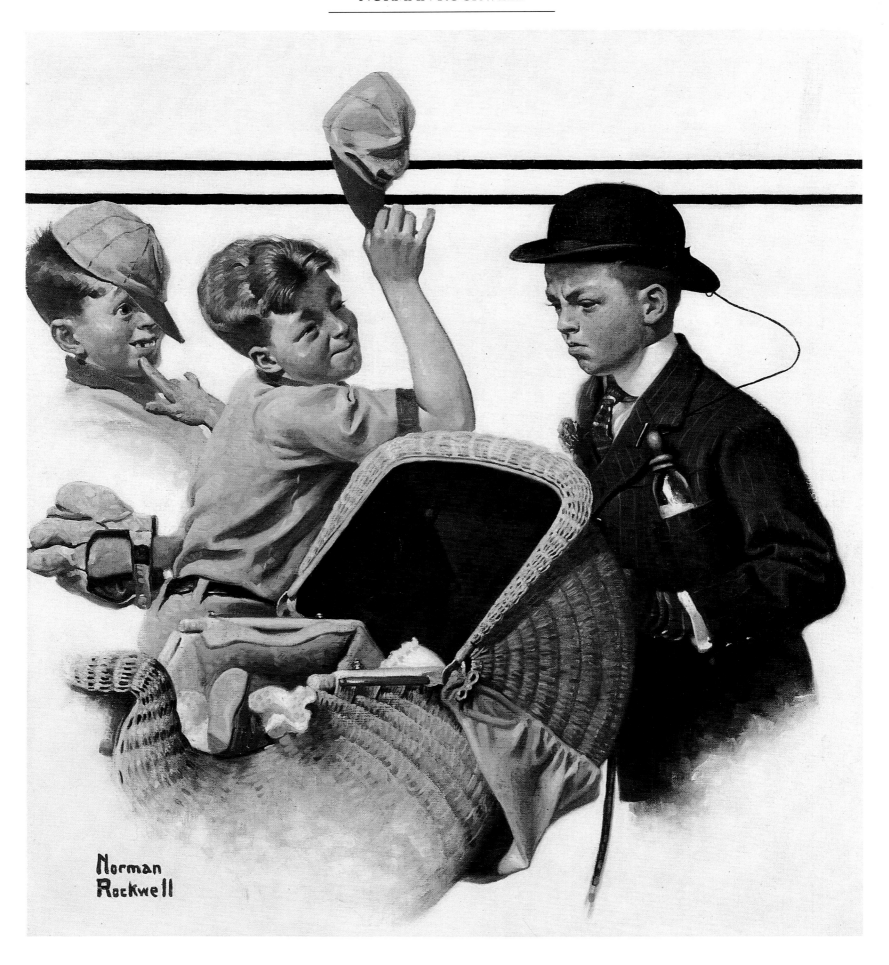

Above: Rockwell's first *Post* cover, *Boy with Carriage* (20 May 1916).

Opposite left: "The Common Cold," part of a series of Rockwell drawings featured in the *Post*, 27 January 1945.

Opposite top right: At times Rockwell found himself in the situation depicted in this *Post* cover, *Artist Faced with Blank Canvas* (8 October 1938).

Opposite bottom right: To get just the right pose, Rockwell often demonstrated the pose himself.

story or the cover. Most of Rockwell's *Post* covers in the 1920s and 1930s, like his first cover, showed an incident. Later during the 1940s, 1950s, and 1960s, many covers featured a scene: the famous series of "Norman Rockwell Visits . . ." fall into this category. This meant that Rockwell could no longer bring everything he needed into the studio: he had to visit an actual country doctor's office, or a ration board, or a country school. That's just what Rockwell did. But as he used photographs more often, he was able to bring images back into his studio. Once he had his idea, Rockwell assembled his props – for the first *Post* cover, this included baseball bats and uniforms, a baby carriage and bottle, and every other item in the picture.

Once the cast of characters and props were assembled, Rockwell made a number of small charcoal sketches of aspects of the scene, and one large charcoal sketch of the entire illustration. Next, he did a rough color painting of the illustration; these paintings were almost impressionistic, compared with Rockwell's final version. Then he was ready to transfer the charcoal sketch to his canvas and begin the finished painting. Rockwell often found himself in the position of working down to the wire: a number of the *Post* covers were delivered before the paint was dry. In fact, several drawings, like the 1938 *Post* cover *Artist Faced with Blank Canvas*, reflected the difficulties he sometimes encountered in meeting a deadline.

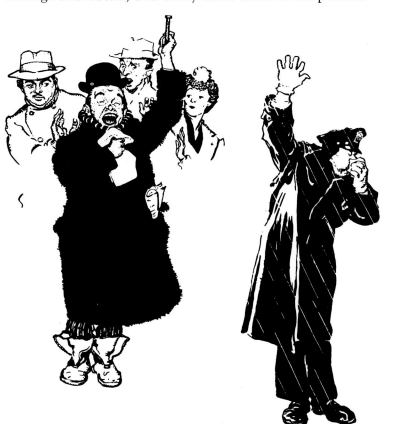

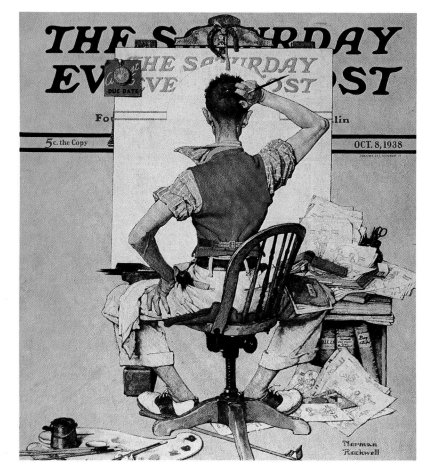

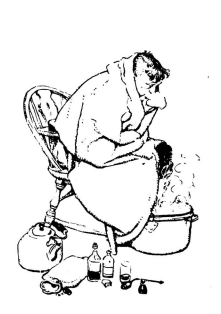

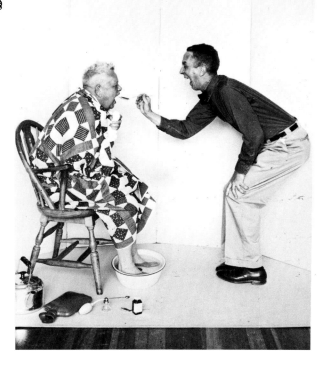

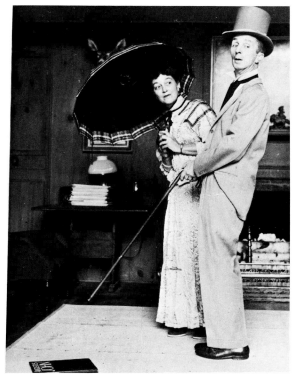

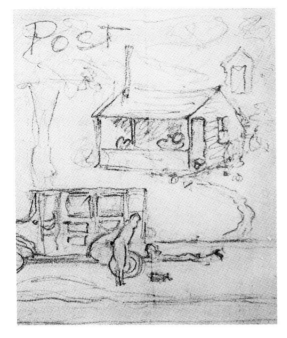

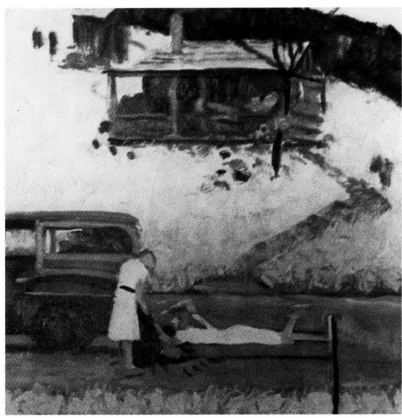

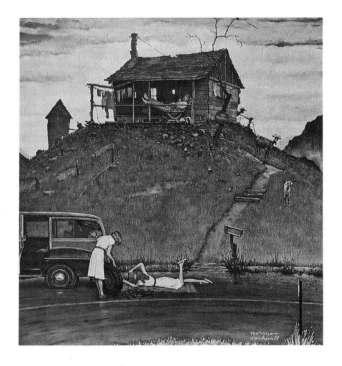

Over the years, as Rockwell's *Post* covers reflected changes in America, they always stressed the positive. In the 1920s Rockwell often featured children and frequently juxtaposed youth and old age, as if to make the point that good times together could overcome any generation gap. In the 1930s Rockwell's cover illustrations sometimes went beyond the edge of the magazine cover, as he experimented with more complex scenes. When the *Post* changed its logo in the 1940s and relegated the magazine's name to the upper left-hand corner of the cover, Rockwell had all the more space for his drawing. The 1940s saw some of Rockwell's most famous covers, focusing on World War II, often through the eyes of Willie Gillis a "typical" G.I. In the 1950s and 1960s Rockwell increasingly did cover portraits for the *Post*, although he continued to commemorate holiday scenes. In many American homes Christmas and Thanksgiving weren't quite official until the *Post* arrived with a Norman Rockwell holiday cover – just as the Boy Scout calendar wasn't itself without one of its 50 years of Rockwell illustrations.

Rockwell's meteoric rise to fame early on brought him the kind of financial stability few illustrators and artists ever achieve. One of the first things he did after selling his first covers to the *Post* in 1916 was to marry Irene O'Connor. The next year, Rockwell decided to enlist in the navy, but when he went for his physical, he was told that he was 17 pounds underweight. It seemed that perhaps Uncle Sam *didn't* want Norman Rockwell for the war effort! However, with the help of a sympathetic navy doctor, Rockwell gorged on doughnuts, bananas, and water, until the scale registered ten extra pounds. The doctor was satisfied, and Norman Rockwell joined the navy, where he served as art editor for *Afloat & Ashore*.

Once out of the navy, Rockwell again submitted most of his work to the *Post*, but in 1924 he was approached by the founders of a new magazine, *Liberty*, which meant to compete with the *Post* and *Colliers*. The *Liberty* art editor tried to woo Rockwell away from the *Post* by promising to double his *Post* cover fee (then $250). Rockwell was sorely tempted, but his loyalties to the *Post* and its editor George Lorimer ran deep. After wrestling inconclusively with his conscience, Rockwell made the familiar journey to the *Post* offices in Philadelphia, and told Lorimer about the offer made by *Liberty*. "Well," said Lorimer, "what are you going to do?" When Rockwell looked at the man who had given him his first big break, he knew what to say; he told Lorimer that he would stay with the *Post*. "All right," Lorimer announced, "*I'll* double your price."

By 1927, Rockwell's marriage was increasingly unhappy, and he made a series of trips without Irene to Europe – a time he later referred to as his "Gertrude Stein and James Joyce period." With a friend, he walked from Munich to Venice, enjoying sketching for his own pleasure with no thought of deadlines or sales. To Rockwell's chagrin, he lost his sketch book near the end of the trip. Years later in referring to his lost sketches, he said: "I've never lost anything I felt so bad about." When Rockwell returned to New Rochelle after a trip in 1929, his wife

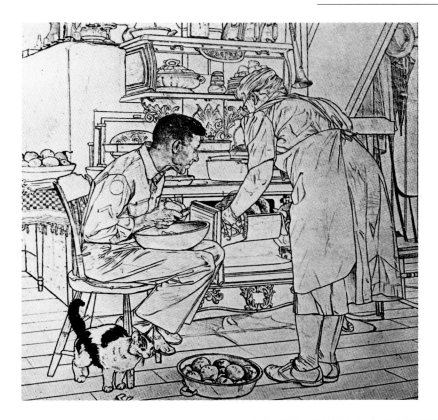

announced that she had filed for divorce, and he moved into bachelor quarters in New York.

Somewhat at loose ends, Rockwell leapt at the chance in 1930 to visit his old friend and fellow artist Clyde Forsythe in Hollywood. There, he met and soon proposed to Mary Barstow, a young teacher. George Lorimer, Rockwell's mentor at the *Post*, was concerned enough about his best illustrator's well-being that he sent novelist Thomas Costaine to California just to check out Rockwell's fiancée; the couple married shortly thereafter. By 1936, the Rockwells had three sons – Jarvis, Thomas, and Peter. It seemed that Rockwell finally had the happy family life he had so often depicted in his illustrations.

Despite his personal happiness, this was a period when Rockwell felt that his work was becoming somewhat stale. So he began to experiment with a new technique called "dynamic symmetry," which had been devised by an illustrator called Jay Hambridge. Basing dynamic symmetry on the mathematical relations of a group of diagrams on an ancient Greek column, Hambridge believed that following certain strict rules of pro-

Above: After searching for the perfect rustic kitchen and models, Rockwell made this detailed drawing for a *Post* Thanksgiving cover. Dissatisfied with the painting, at the last minute Rockwell redid the scene, using other models. For the final version, see page 69.

Opposite: Typical of his working method, Rockwell made a number of charcoal sketches and a rough color painting before executing the final version of *Fixing a Flat*.

Right: Examples of Rockwell's sketches of Paris made during his 1932 European trip.

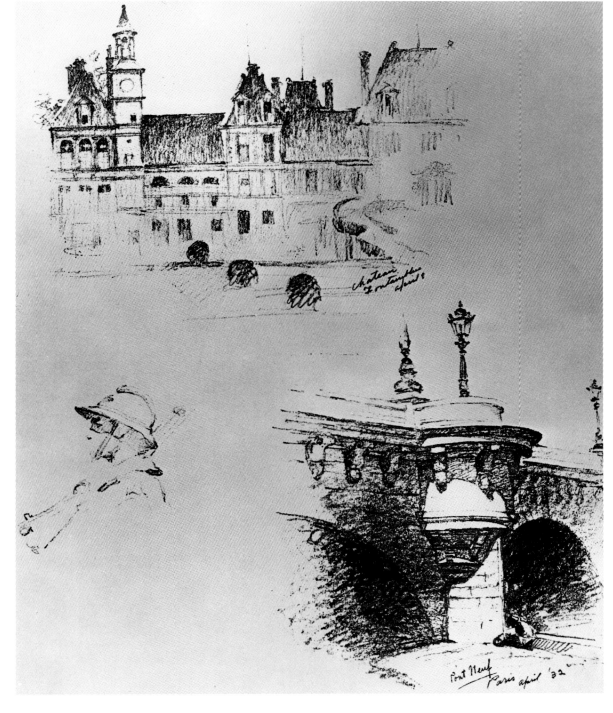

13

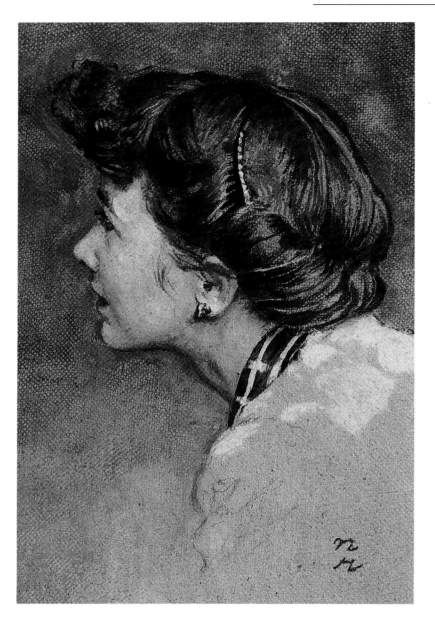

portion produced the finest drawings. Rockwell's only *Post* cover using this technique was not a success, and he subsequently sank into a depression, almost unable to work.

Even Rockwell's usual panacea, a spur-of-the-moment trip to Europe, did nothing to dispel his paralysis. Interestingly, none of Rockwell's inner turmoil was reflected in his *Post* covers, or in the superb work he did illustrating *Tom Sawyer* and *Huckleberry Finn* for the Heritage Press. In fact, Rockwell's work illustrating Mark Twain books helped to sustain him through depression; in times of stress, he found it easier to illustrate someone else's work than to come up with his own ideas. However, he preferred to paint his own ideas, which he thought of as "storytelling pictures."

Months passed before Rockwell was once more working comfortably. Matters were not helped when George Lorimer (who had become something of a father figure) left the *Post*, and was replaced by Wesley Stout, with whom Rockwell never felt at ease. Nevertheless, Rockwell's work continued to appear regularly in the *Post*. In 1939 Rockwell decided that he had had enough of New Rochelle and moved his family to a quintessential "Norman Rockwell" village in Arlington, Vermont. Soon, Rockwell mentally catalogued several hundred Arlington inhabitants as models and was working with more pleasure than he had in years. Arlington was where Rockwell did some of his best-known work: the "Willie Gillis G.I." *Post* cover series and in 1943, the *Four Freedoms*, initially published as inside features in the *Post*. Sent coast to coast and reproduced as posters by the Treasury Department, the *Four Freedoms* inspired war bond sales of $132,992,539.

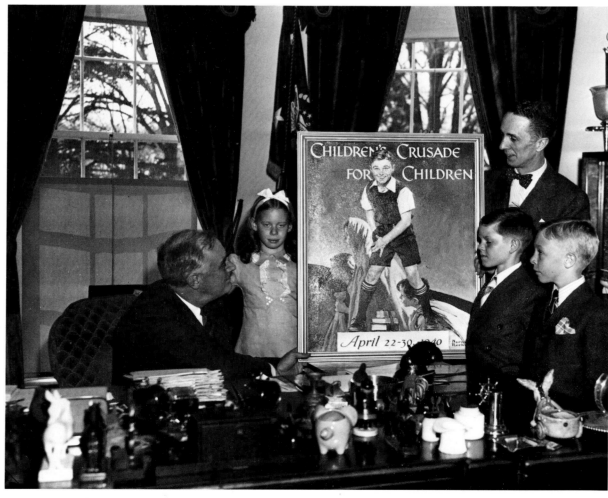

Opposite above: Portrait of Mary Barstow Rockwell, who married Rockwell in 1930.

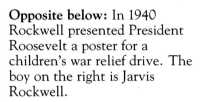

Opposite below: In 1940 Rockwell presented President Roosevelt a poster for a children's war relief drive. The boy on the right is Jarvis Rockwell.

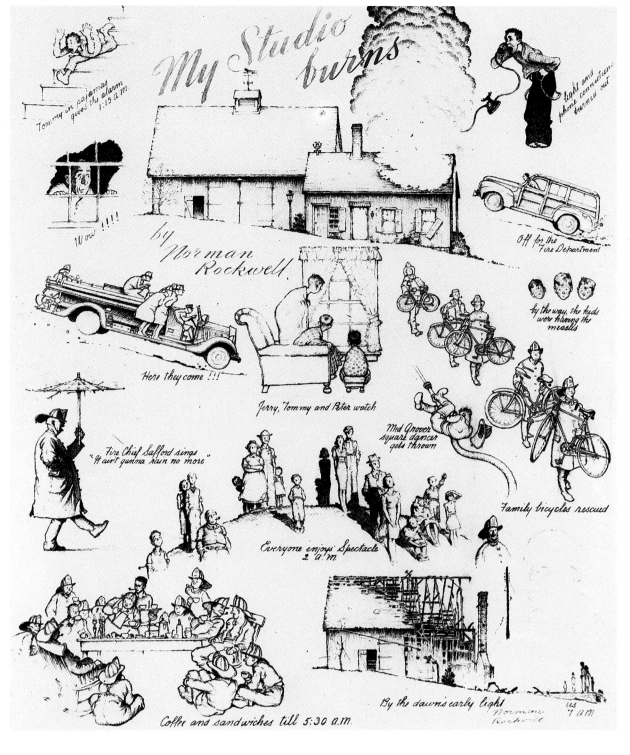

Right: "My Studio Burns" relates the events of the night in 1943 when Rockwell's Arlington studio was destroyed in a fire.

In short, Rockwell's career was on track again; but just as he seemed to have a new lease on his career, disaster struck. One night, Rockwell's Arlington studio – with all his paintings, his collection of Howard Pyle sketches, and his extensive collection of costumes and props – burnt to the ground. Rockwell realized that he had lost "everything, the accumulation of twenty-eight years of painting, traveling, collecting." What made matters worse was Rockwell's admission that the fire had been his own fault; ashes from his pipe had caused the blaze. Within days, Rockwell and his wife decided to move down the road to West Arlington, where the studio was rebuilt with the help of neighbors.

Before long Rockwell was back working and enjoying his three sons, who swam and fished in a nearby creek and attended West Arlington's one-room school on the green. Yet, by 1953, Rockwell was once again restless and depressed; it was time for another move, this time to West Stockbridge, Massachusetts,

where he was able to take advantage of the psychiatrists at the Austin Riggs Center, especially the famous psychoanalyst Erik H. Erickson.

By the time he arrived in Stockbridge, Rockwell was almost as much of a celebrity as many of the politicians and movie stars he painted. Increasingly, unwanted visitors haunted Main Street, and turned up at Rockwell's studio to ask for an autograph or to watch the famous illustrator at work. One day, Rockwell took pity on a large group of women peering curiously up at his studio, and invited them in. As he later put it, "That was one helluva mistake!" Sometime after Rockwell thought he had finally shooed away his visitors, he found one determined woman in the back of the studio, still looking through his sketches. After that, Mary Rockwell increasingly ran interference on the telephone and at the house to protect Rockwell's privacy.

When Mary died suddenly at 51 of a heart attack in 1959,

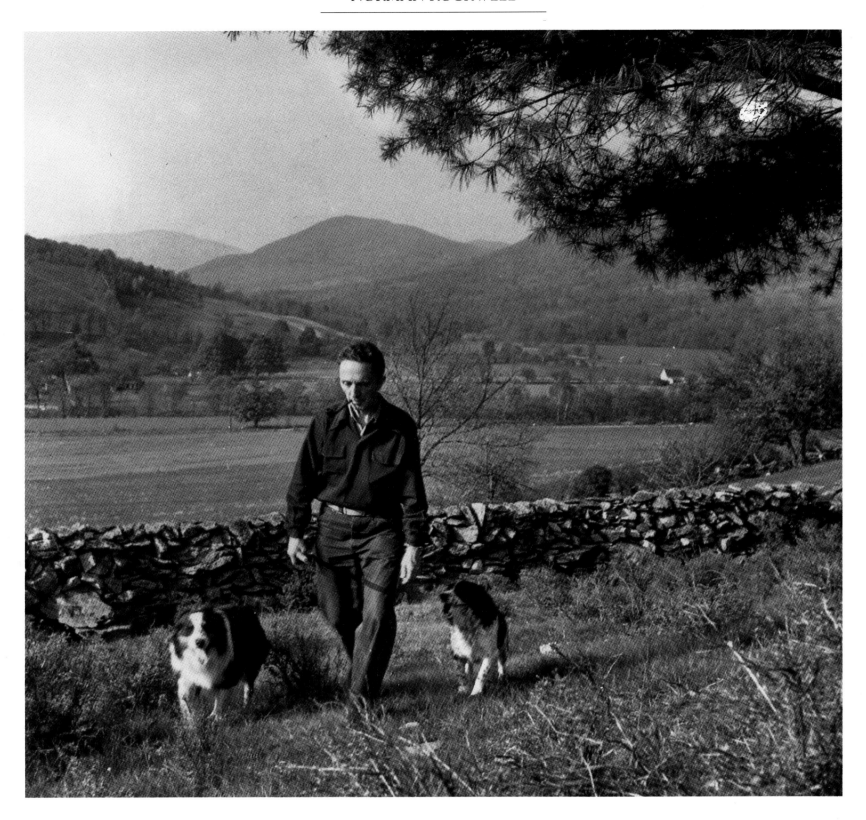

Rockwell was shattered; he was 65, his wife was dead, and his sons were grown and no longer at home. A visit the next year to Grandma Moses on her 100th birthday helped to convince Rockwell that his best days need not be behind him, but this was still a period of artistic stagnation. Somewhat at loose ends, Rockwell wrote his autobiography, *My Adventures as an Illustrator*, in collaboration with his son Thomas. It was not until he met and married Molly Punderson, a retired school teacher, in 1961, that Rockwell returned wholeheartedly to his work.

By 1963, Rockwell illustrations had been appearing in the *Post* for 47 years, averaging per year six or seven covers and numerous story illustrations. He was fiercely loyal to the *Post*, which never paid him more than $5000 for a cover (less than half of what he made from other clients for a painting). Yet in the 1960s, the *Post* was beginning to run into circulation prob-

lems, and in 1963, the editors decided to adopt a new cover format, using photographs instead of drawings. The decision spelled the end of Norman Rockwell covers for the *Post*. His last cover, showing the recently assassinated President Kennedy, appeared in December of 1963.

When *Look* magazine approached Rockwell the next year, he was glad for the chance to continue working – although he by no means needed the income. Unlike the *Post*, which had always prided itself on its fiction – by writers like Shirley Jackson and John O'Hara, whose work often appeared in the influential *New Yorker* – *Look* concentrated on non-fiction feature stories. As a result, Rockwell, at age 70, had to turn away from his warm-hearted depictions of Americana and illustrate important news events. Although Rockwell did the bulk of his work for *Look* during the next decade, he continued to submit nostalgic holiday and genre scenes to magazines like *McCall's*.

Rockwell's first drawing for *Look* after he stopped working for the *Post* was a stunning departure from his earlier work: *The Problem We All Live With* showed a determined young black girl, escorted by burly U.S. marshalls, trying to ignore a hostile crowd of segregationists as she goes off to attend a formerly all-white school. Deliberately, Rockwell did not show the crowd, whose presence is indicated by the blood-red smear of a recently thrown tomato and the graffiti "Nigger" on the wall behind. Nor did he show the faces of the marshalls, in order to increase the focus on the young girl herself.

The painting – in subject and technique – was a startling switch for the man who had always said that he painted life as

Opposite: After the fire in Arlington, Rockwell moved to West Arlington. Here, he continued to enjoy the Vermont countryside, often with the Labrador retrievers that he bred.

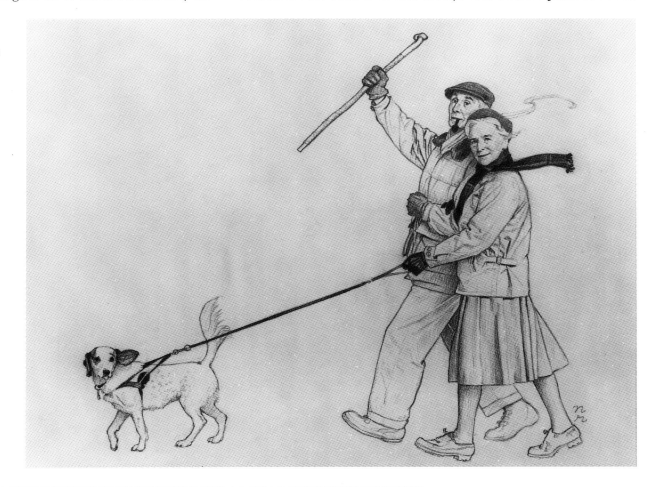

Right: In 1961 Rockwell married Molly Punderson, a former teacher at Milton Academy Girls School. Molly is shown here in a Christmas card drawn by Rockwell.

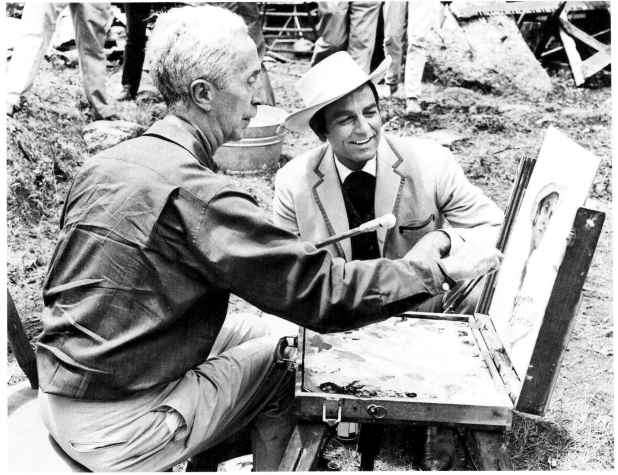

Left: In 1966 Martin Rackin, producer of the 20th Century-Fox release *Stagecoach*, commissioned Rockwell to paint pictures of the film for publicity, including this portrait of actor Mike Connors.

he would like it to be. Now Rockwell was painting the dark side of America; furthermore, the painting was an editorial in words: the artist's sympathies were with the young girl, and the painting was meant to evoke the sympathies of the viewer. For years, Rockwell had invited viewers to chuckle with him at the antics of children; now he was inviting them to share his shame in *The Problem We All Live With*. Three years later, Rockwell again tackled the subject of integration for *Look*, this time in a more characteristically "Rockwell" manner: *New Kids in the Neighborhood* showed two neighborhood "old kids," both white, eyeing the two "new kids," both black children, standing beside a moving van. The mood, however, is of hope, and the scene seems to depict the moment just before one of the four children breaks the ice by asking, "What's your name?"

During the 1960s, Rockwell and his wife Molly traveled the world for *Look*, bringing back paintings from India, Russia, and Europe, of world leaders and "the man in the street." Just as America had once watched itself through Rockwell's eyes, now Rockwell was offering a window on the world, combining his genius for photographic realism with his affectionate insights into human character. In America, Rockwell's own celebrity meant that he spent increasing amounts of time doing celebrity portraits, including presidents and political candidates, as well as many of Hollywood's best-known actors. In 1965 Rockwell traveled to Hollywood to paint the stars of Twentieth Century Fox's forthcoming film *Stagecoach* and was delighted to be offered a bit part in the movie, appearing along with Ann-Margret, Bing Crosby, Robert Cummings, Van Heflin, Slim Pickens and Red Buttons. It was a considerable part of Rockwell's charm that, all his life, he was thrilled to meet the famous – and never quite believed in his *own* fame.

By the 1970s, even the prodigiously energetic Rockwell was slowing down a little, taking on fewer commissions. In addition, many of the companies for which he had done advertisements were using photographs, and many of the magazines for which he had done his best work, like the *Post*, were defunct. Rockwell, and the *Post* itself, seemed to be a part of the past, but he found himself once more in the public eye in 1972 when New York's Bernard Danenberg Galleries mounted a 65-year retrospective of his work. Predictably, the critics were less than generous in their appraisal of Rockwell, whom they had never taken seriously as an artist. For the most part, this was just fine with Rockwell, who always prided himself on his craft as an illustrator, and slyly hinted on *Post* covers like *Artist and Critic* and *The Connoisseur* that "serious" art was not his cup of tea.

In fact, Rockwell admitted in his autobiography that he couldn't paint "world-shaking ideas" and clearly saw his talent as doing "ordinary people in everyday situations, and that's about all I can do." In addition, Rockwell was unabashed in admitting that much of twentieth-century art – from the 1913 Armory Show right through late Picasso – had had no effect whatsoever on his technique. In addition, like most illustrators, Rockwell's work was explicit, not interpretative: in most Rockwells the "story" takes precedence over form, and the

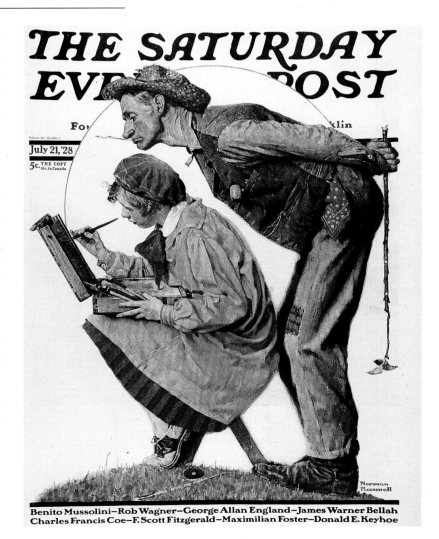

Benito Mussolini–Rob Wagner–George Allan England–James Warner Bellah
Charles Francis Coe–F. Scott Fitzgerald–Maximilian Foster–Donald E. Keyhoe

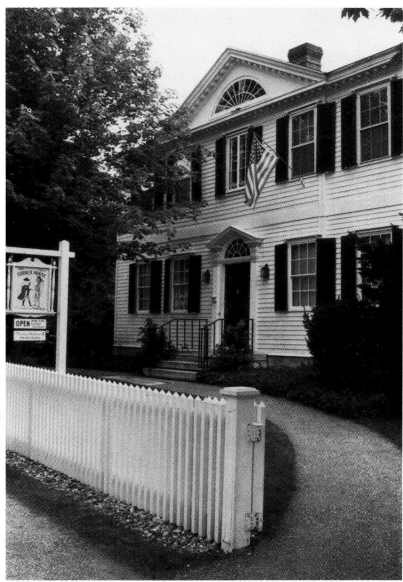

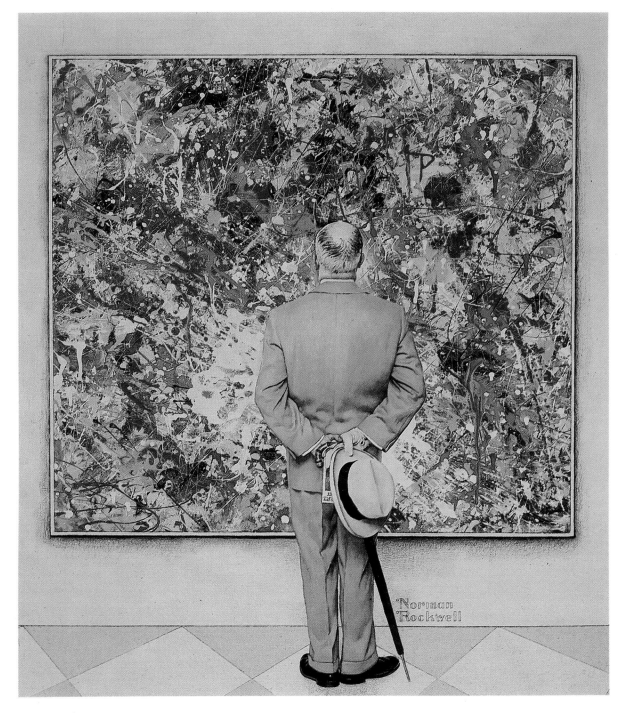

Opposite above and left:
Rockwell took pride in being
an illustrator and slyly hinted
in *Post* covers, such as *Artist
and Critic* (21 July 1928) and
The Connoisseur (13 January
1962), that "serious" art was
not his cup of tea.

Opposite below: Since the
1970s, the Norman Rockwell
Museum at Stockbridge has
exhibited the artist's work.
Soon the collection will be
rehoused in a new Rockwell
museum in Stockbridge.

Below: In preparing the
splattered canvas for the
background of *The Connoisseur*,
Rockwell used Jackson Pollack's
"dribble" method, proving that
he, too, could paint in a
modern style. (Photo by Louie
Lamone.)

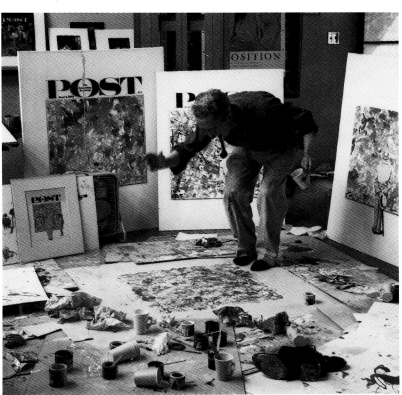

narrative is immediately intelligible, never mysterious and
haunting.

If Rockwell was disappointed by the critics' reaction to his
1972 retrospective, he was heartened to realize that his public
had by no means forgotten him. Thus he decided to preserve
his art collection at The Old Corner House Museum in Stockbridge, Massachusetts. In 1976 Rockwell painted his last cover,
for the bicentennial edition of *American Artist* magazine, and
the next year he received the Presidential Medal of Freedom for
his "vivid and affectionate portraits of this country." Norman
Rockwell, who once admitted that "I have always wanted
everybody to like my work," died at his home in Stockbridge on
8 November 1978. For more than six decades, almost everybody in America *did* like Rockwell, whose work remains a
national family album of sorts for millions of Americans; soon
his collection will be rehoused in Stockbridge's new Norman
Rockwell Museum. Perhaps Rockwell himself summed up his
contribution best when he said, "I showed the America I knew
and observed to others who might not have noticed."

HUMAN INTEREST

Norman Rockwell realized that his talent lay in showing "ordinary people in everyday situations," and he was always on the lookout for the right model to heighten the human interest in his paintings. The reason that Norman Rockwell's people look like real people is that they *were* real people – wearing real pirate costumes, threading real needles, holding real ice cream cones, and sitting in real airplanes or rumbleseats. In the early days in New Rochelle when most of Rockwell's work was for *Boys' Life*, he made frequent expeditions to school yards and playgrounds to find child models. Usually the boys were eager to model when they learned that Rockwell paid $.50 an hour; if they were cool to the idea, Rockwell knew how to win over their mothers by dangling the prospect of seeing their son's face in a national magazine.

It was never easy to convince active young boys to sit still during a modeling session. The method with which Rockwell had the most success was stacking the boy's fee in nickles alongside his easel. Every 30 minutes, he would push five of the nickles aside, so that the young model could see his earnings grow. Even this didn't prevent the boys from organizing water fights in the studio whenever Rockwell's back was turned. Nor were boy models Rockwell's only problem: since many of the *Boys' Life* illustrations featured "a boy and his dog," he spent a good deal of time chasing appealing mutts around New Rochelle. Some of his neighbors suspected him of being a vivisectionist; others, Rockwell recalled, thought he was "just crazy."

Things got a bit easier when Rockwell discovered Billy Paine, who had such an India-rubber face that he could manage almost any expression – as demonstrated by Paine's appearance as all three boys on Rockwell's first *Post* cover, *Boy with Carriage*. Years later, Rockwell described Billy as "the best kid model I ever had." Unfortunately, Billy came to no good end: the boy whom Rockwell thought of as a "regular rapscallion" fell to his death at 13, falling out of a window with a ladies girdle which he had stolen as a prank. Rockwell's favorite girl model was Mary Whalen, who posed for the 1952 *Post* cover *Day in the Life of a Little Girl*. Whalen won Rockwell's heart by her ability to raise her eyebrows like two parentheses, almost as high as her hair line, in Rockwell's favorite expression of surprise.

After 1916, as Rockwell began doing more and more work for the *Post*, he needed a wider range of models. One of his favorites in the 1920s was James Van Brunt, whose luxurious eight-inch long mustache appeared on so many *Post* covers that the editors persuaded Rockwell to make Van Brunt shave; sadly, once the mustache was gone, Van Brunt was revealed as having a rabbity upper lip, which Rockwell then had to hide in his paintings. Worse, when the mustache grew back, it was scraggly, and never regained its former glory. In addition to Van Brunt, some of Rockwell's favorite models in the New Rochelle days were former actors, like James Wilson and Pop Fredericks, with their own extensive collections of costumes. Many other models, like news agent Dave Campion were simply locals whom Rockwell had noticed and asked to pose. When Rockwell used Campion and Fredericks, along with a boy named Billy Sundermeyer, in his 1924 *Post* cover *Christmas ... Sing Merrilie*, he was amused that all three were virtually tone deaf.

By the time that Rockwell was living in Arlington, Vermont, and Stockbridge, Massachusetts, his fame was such that almost everyone was flattered to be asked to model, and many would have paid for the privilege. It's a sign of Rockwell's talent for portraying real people in familiar situations, that visitors to Stockbridge's Old Corner House frequently ask "what ever happened to" a character from a favorite Rockwell *Post* cover, and speculate as to how old someone like the 1954 *Post* cover *Girl at the Mirror* would be today. Rockwell's particular genius lay in his ability to make people care about his real models, while identifying with the characters and situations those models portrayed. Rockwell always said that he painted "storytelling pictures"; the stories the pictures tell are as full of human interest today as they were when Rockwell painted them.

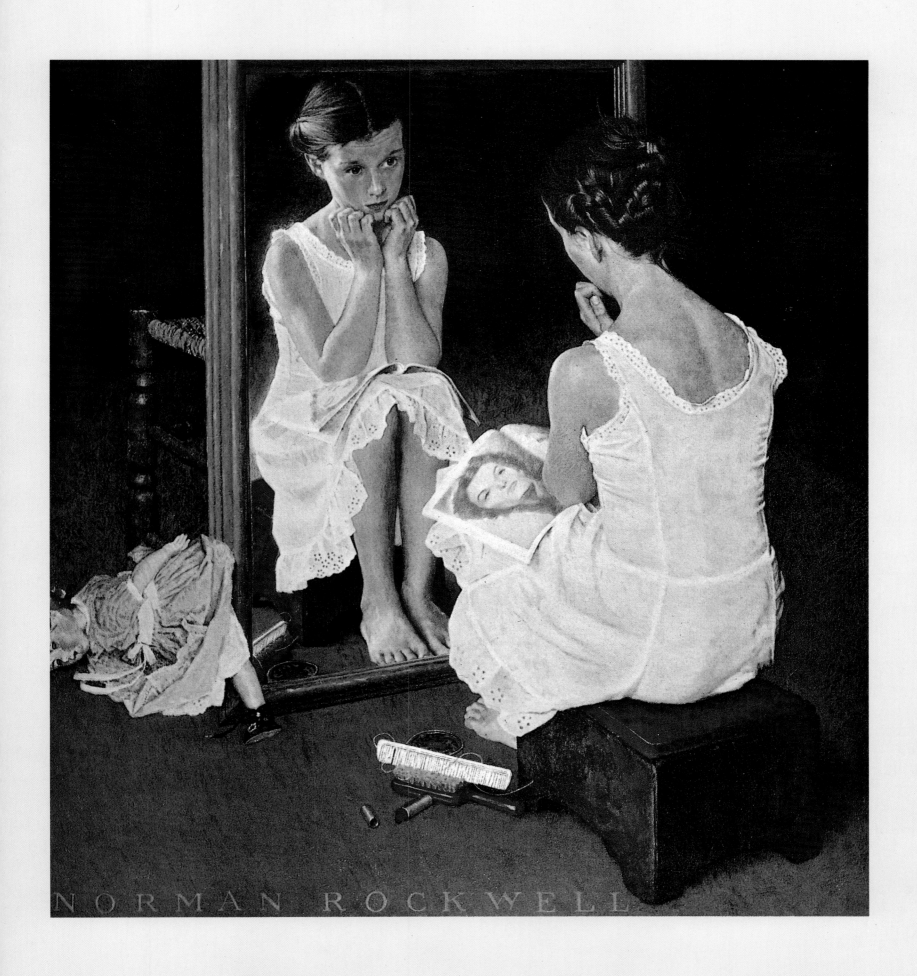

Girl at the Mirror
Original oil painting for a *Post* cover, 6 March 1954

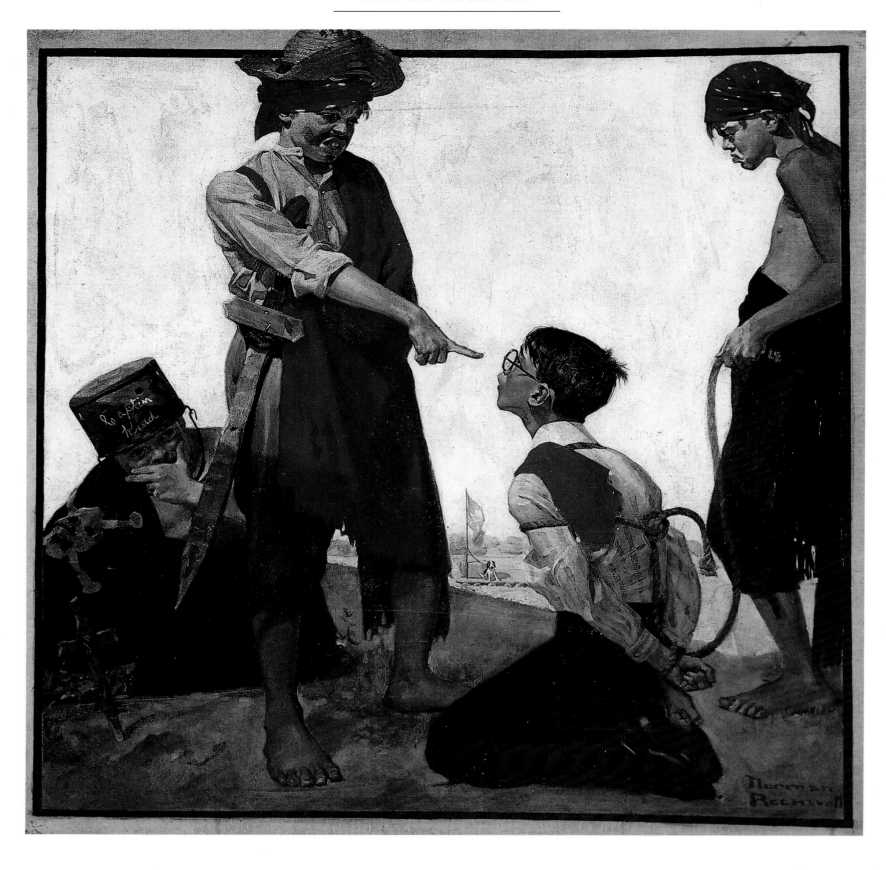

Cousin Reginald Plays Pirate
Country Gentleman cover, 3 November 1917

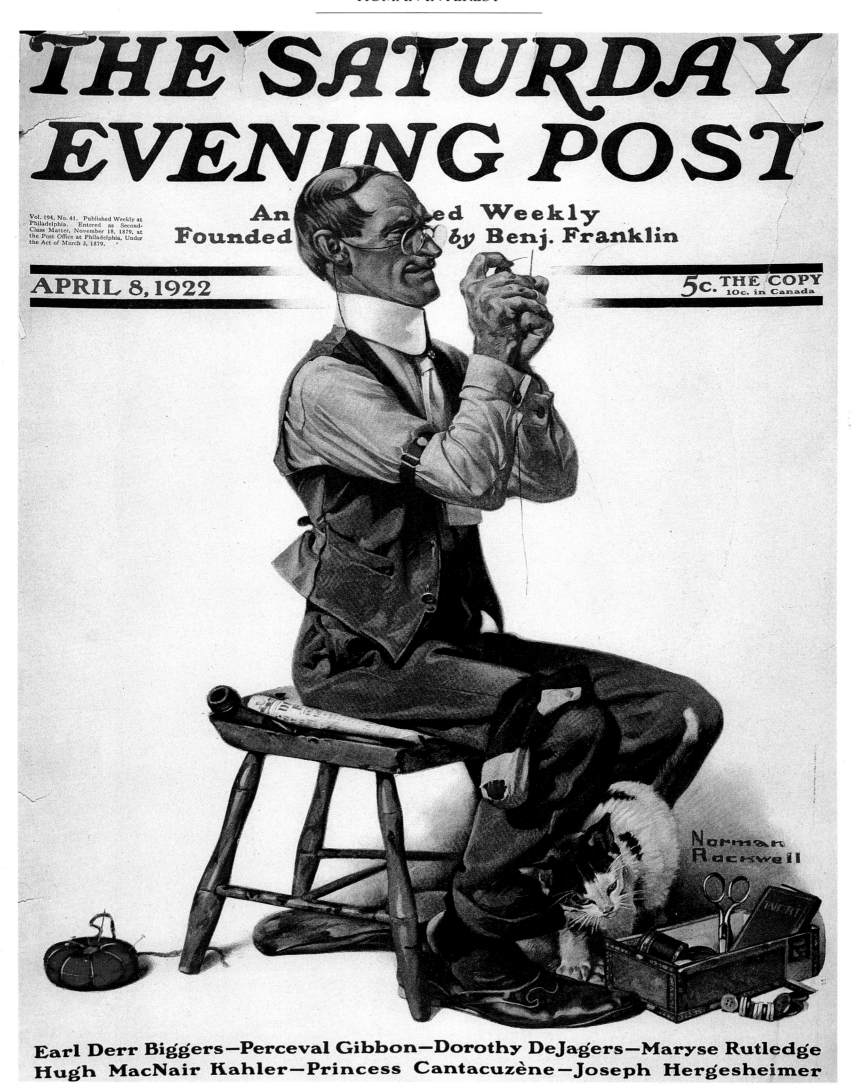

Man Threading Needle
Post cover, 8 April 1922

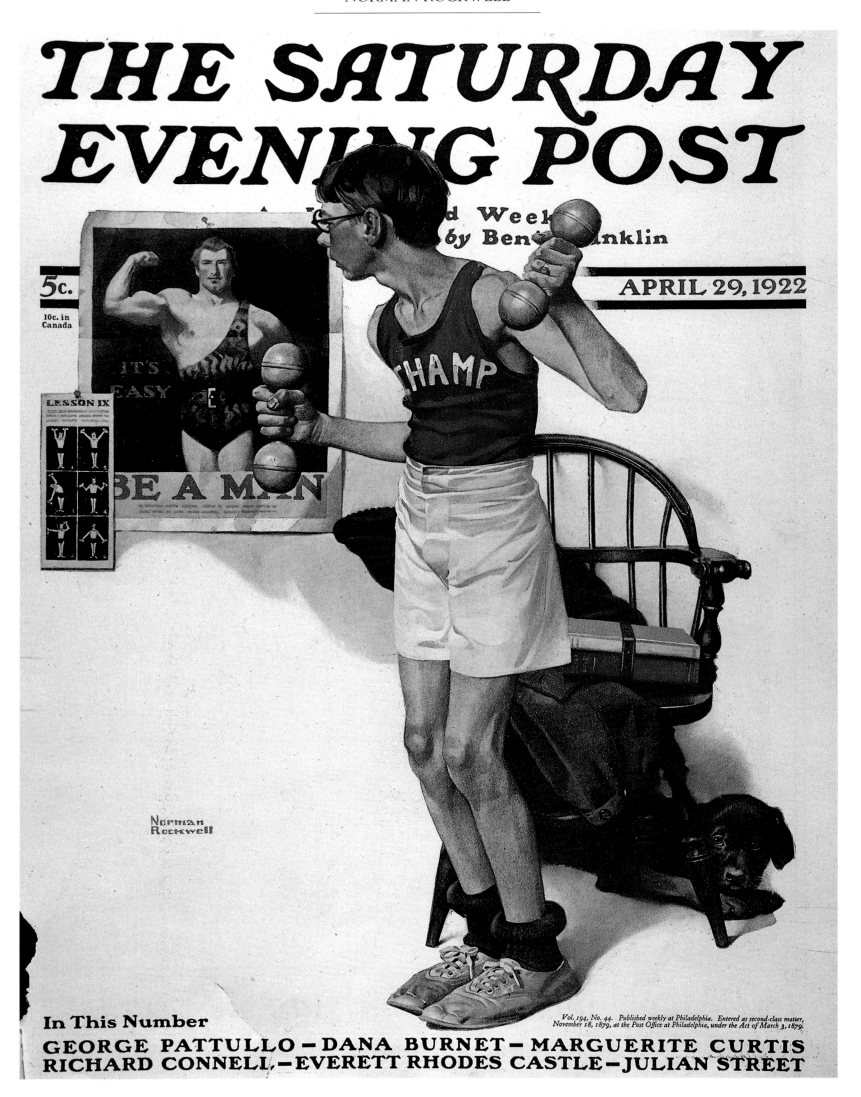

The Bodybuilder
Post cover, 29 April 1922

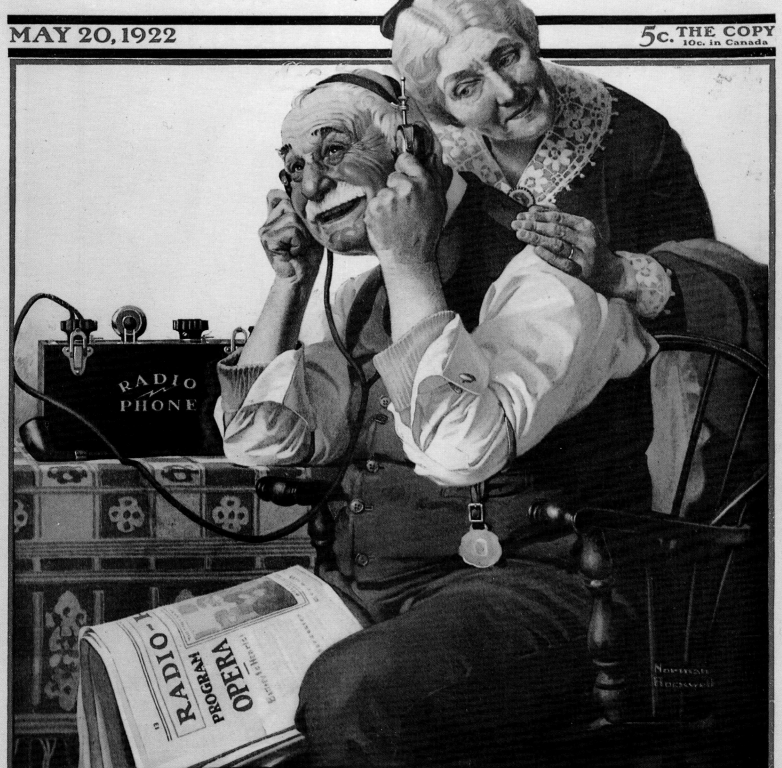

The Wonders of Radio
Post cover, 20 May 1922

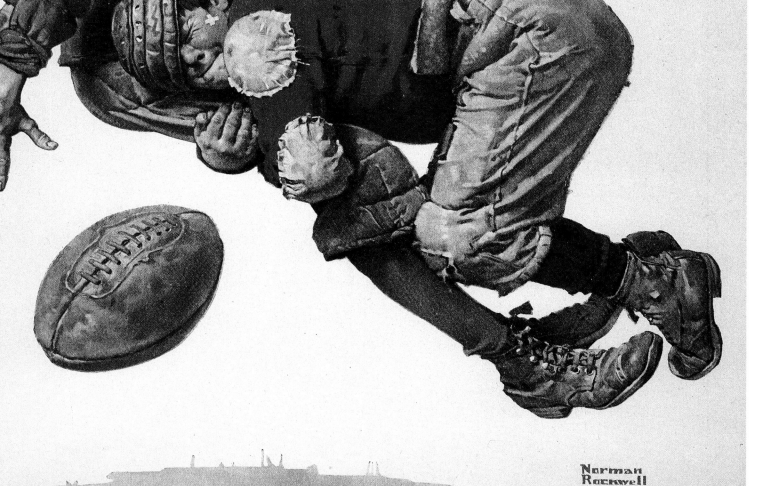

Tackled
Post cover, 21 November 1925

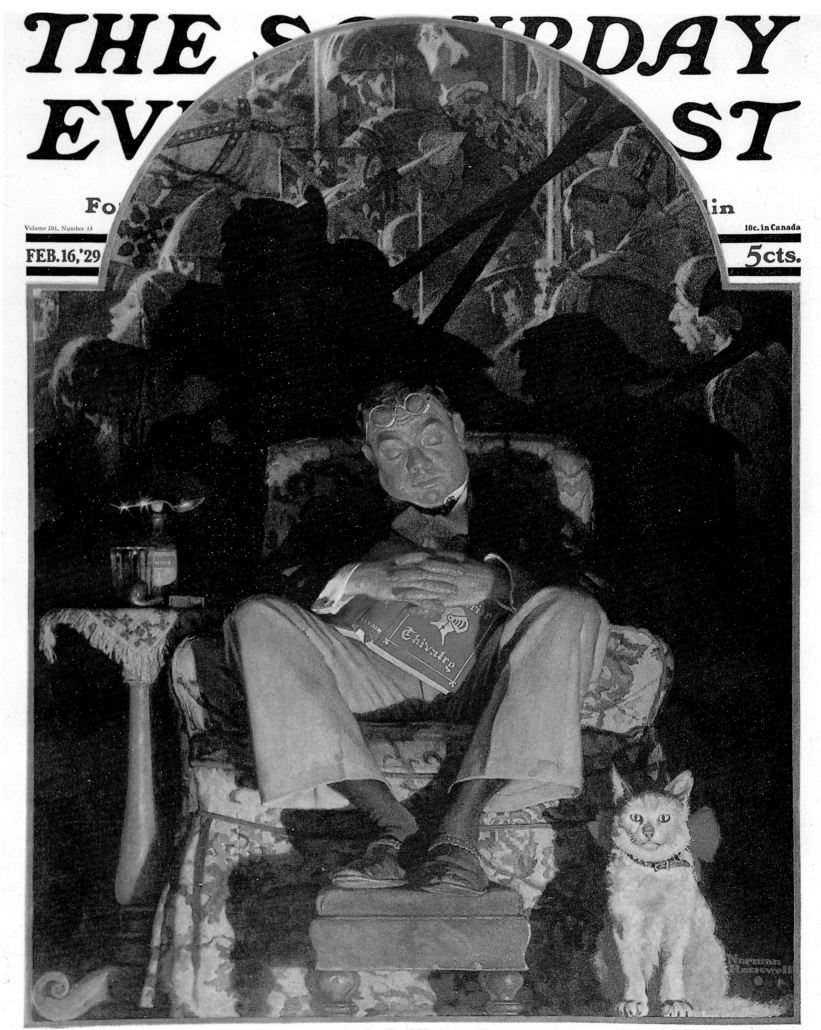

Dreams of Chivalry
Post cover, 16 February 1929

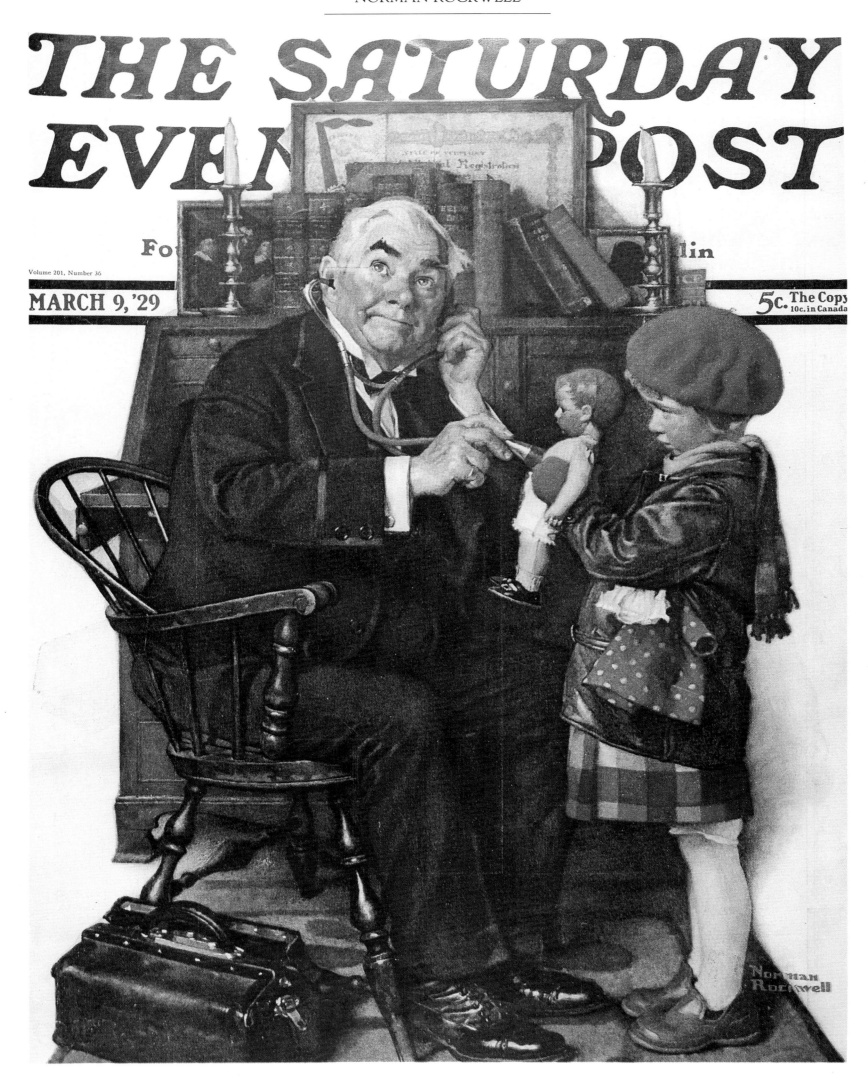

Doctor and Doll
Post cover, 9 March 1929

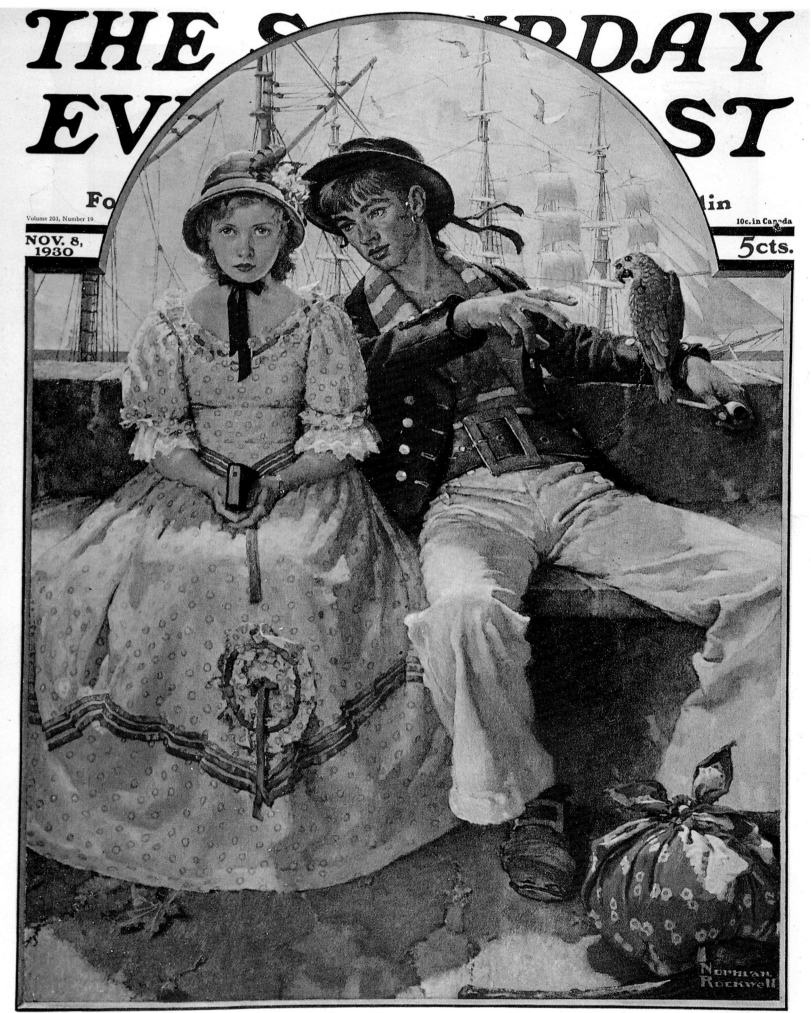

The Yarn Spinner
Post cover, 8 November 1930

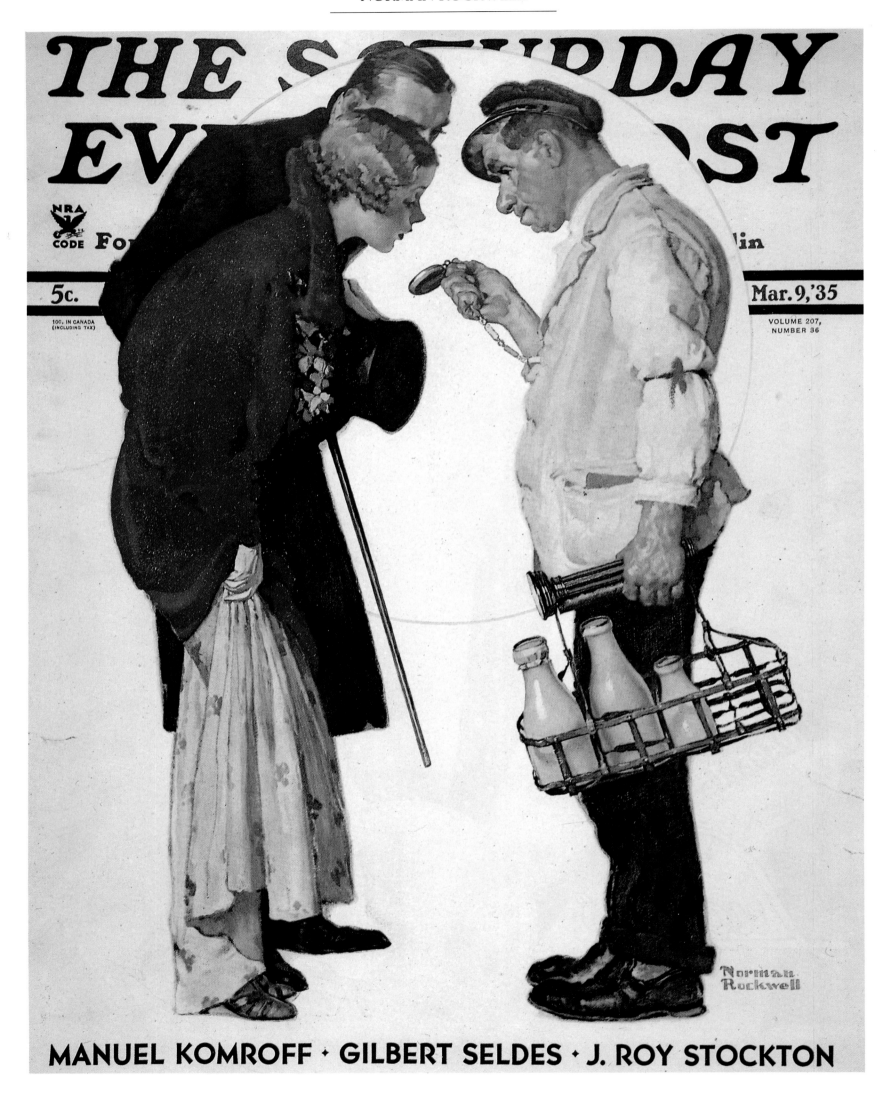

The Partygoers
Post cover, 9 March 1935

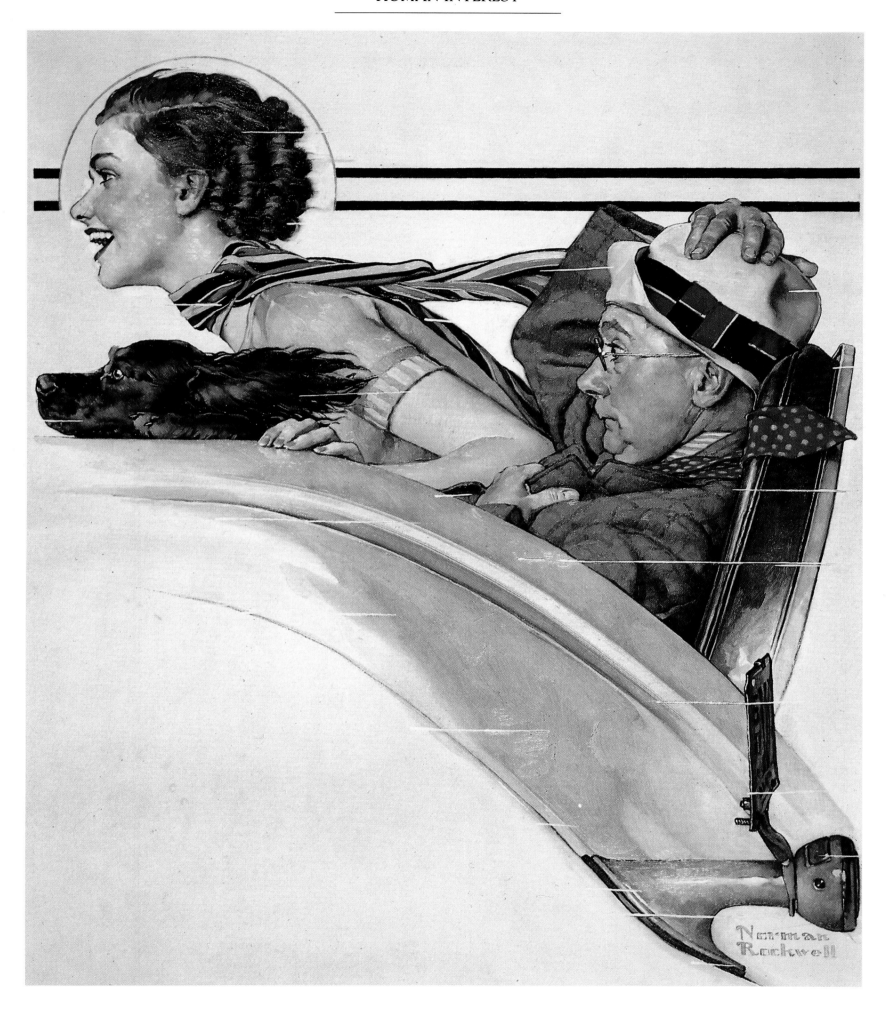

Couple in Rumbleseat
Original oil painting for a *Post* cover, 13 July 1935

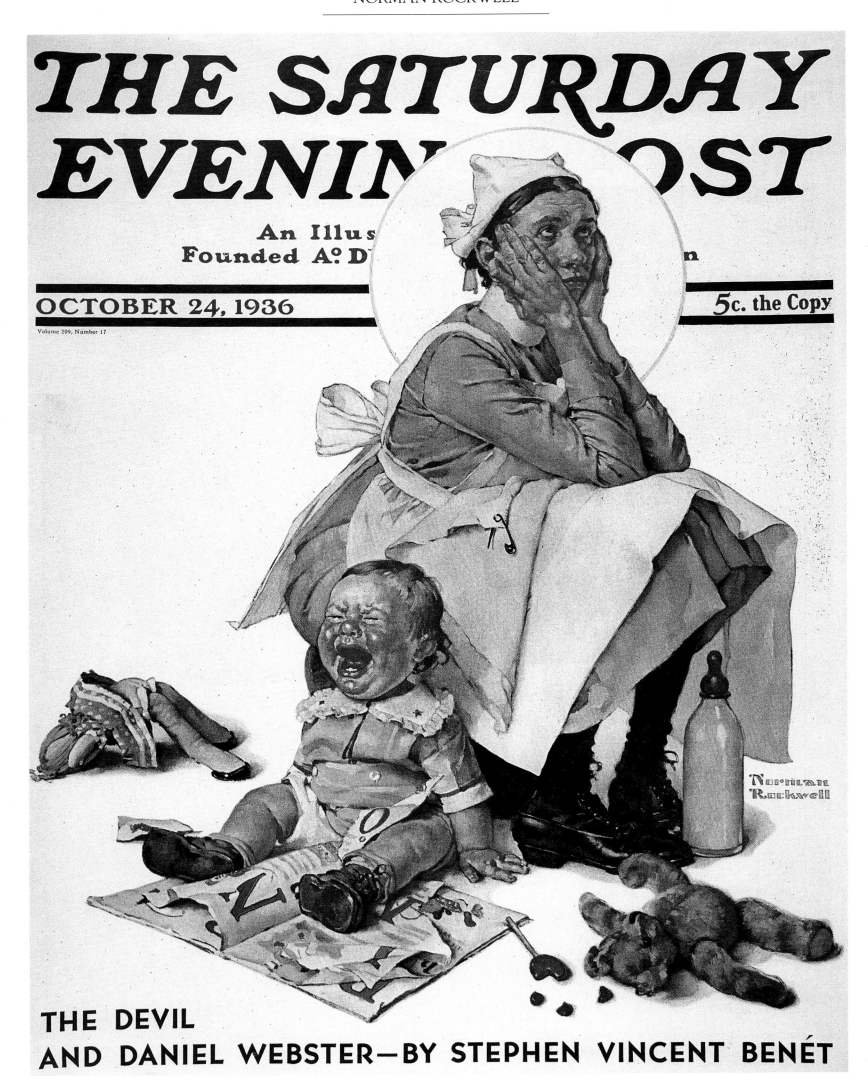

THE SATURDAY EVENING POST

An Illus...
Founded A⁰ D...

OCTOBER 24, 1936

Volume 209, Number 17

5c. the Copy

Norman Rockwell

**THE DEVIL
AND DANIEL WEBSTER—BY STEPHEN VINCENT BENÉT**

The Tantrum
Post cover, 24 October 1936

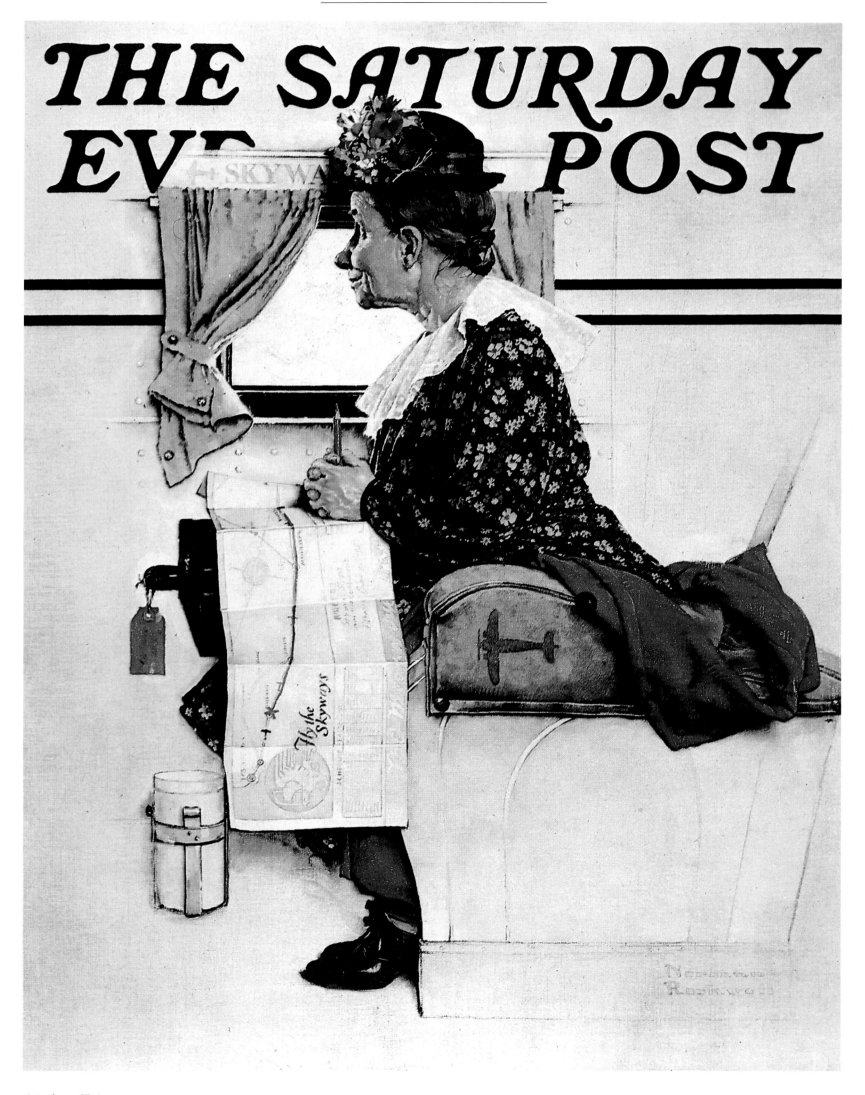

Airplane Trip
Original oil painting for a *Post* cover, 4 June 1938

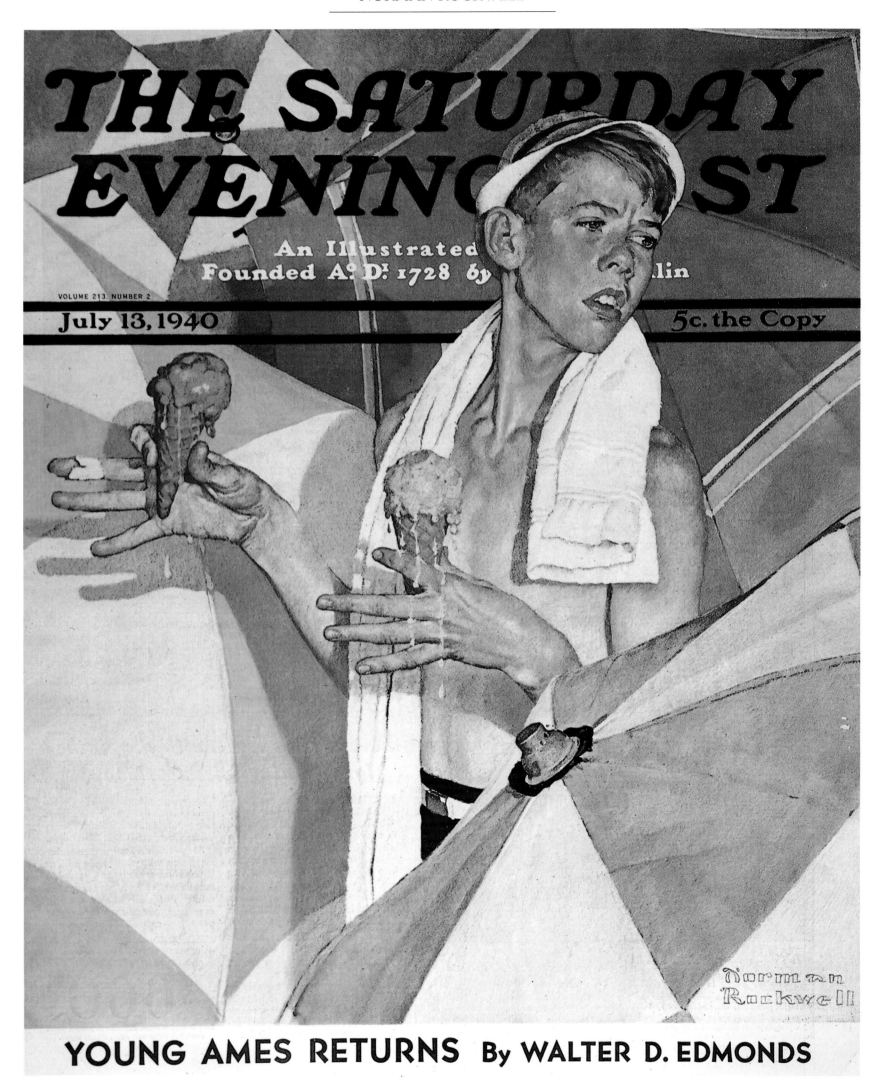

Ice Cream Carrier
Post cover, 13 July 1940

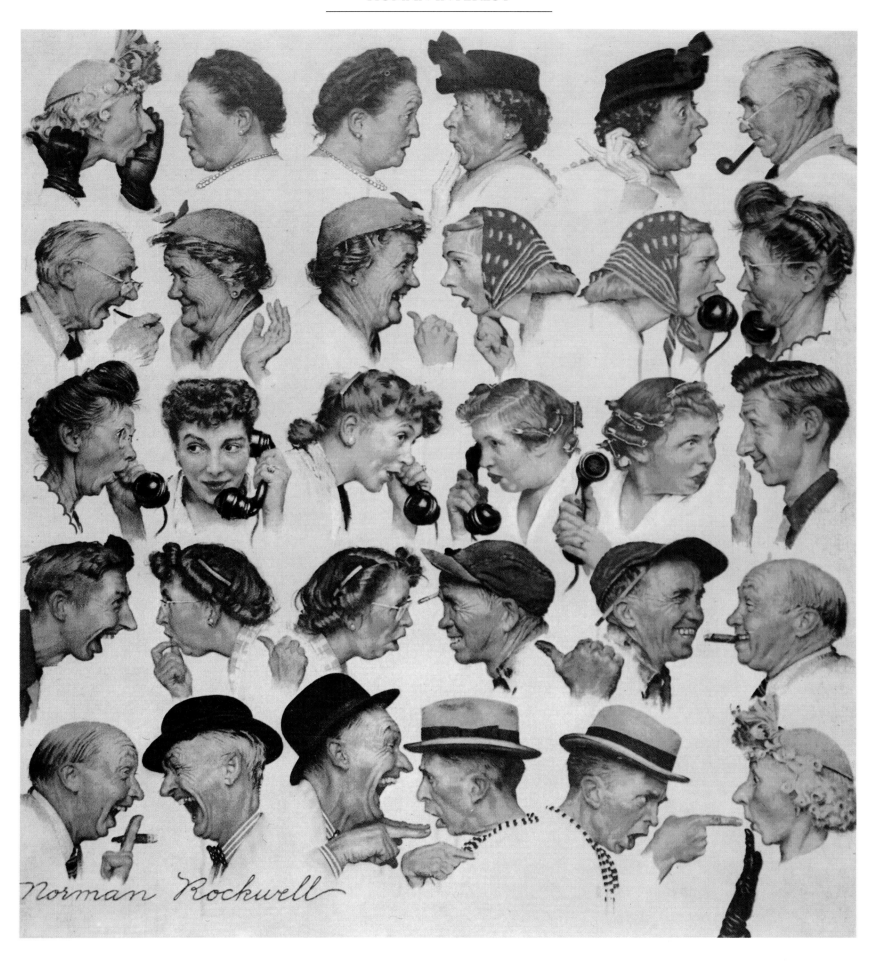

The Gossips
Post cover, 6 March 1948

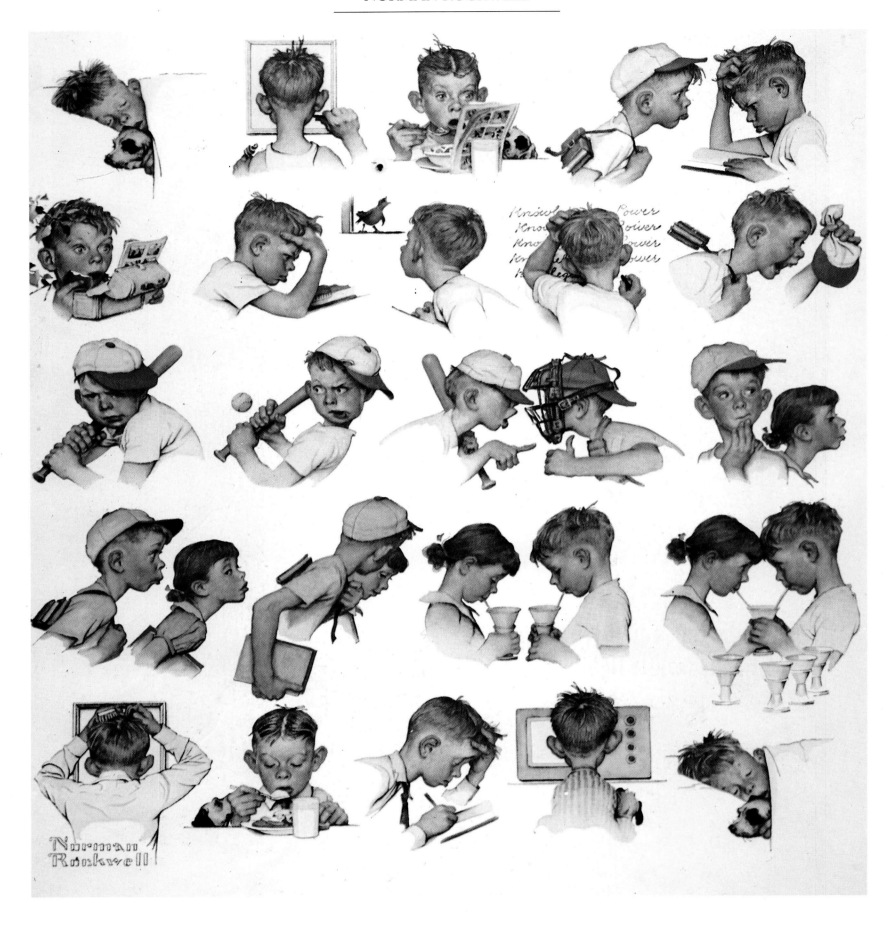

Day in the Life of a Little Boy
Post cover, 24 May 1952

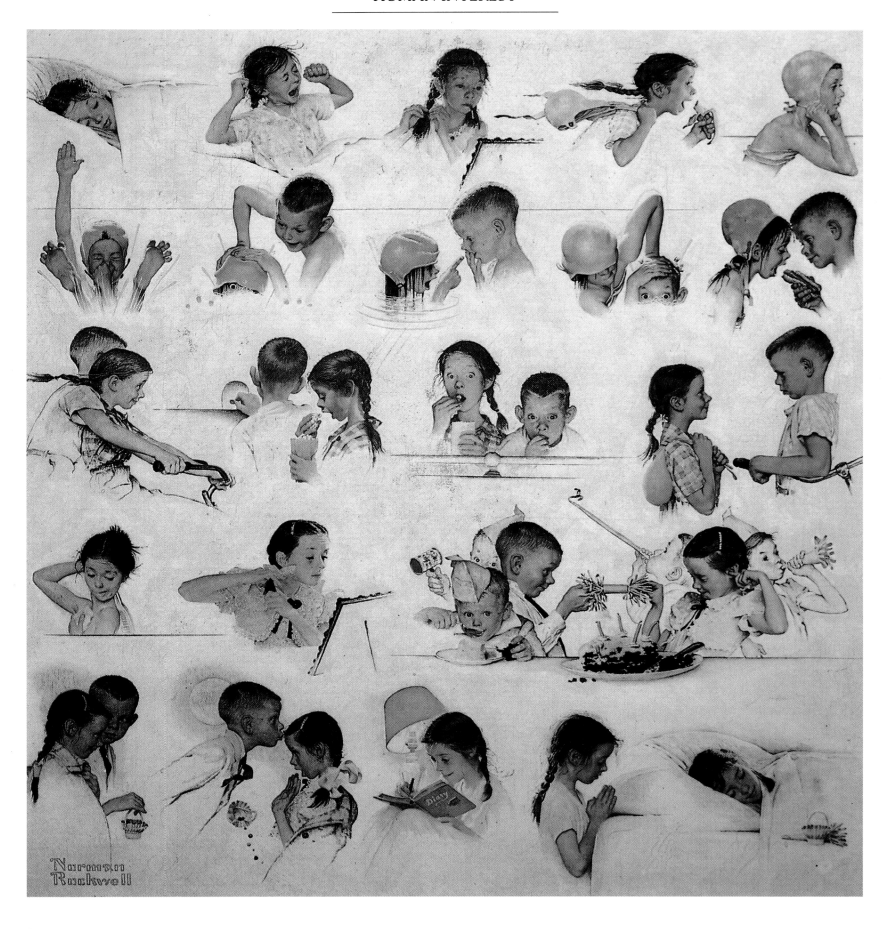

Day in the Life of a Little Girl
Post cover, 30 August 1952

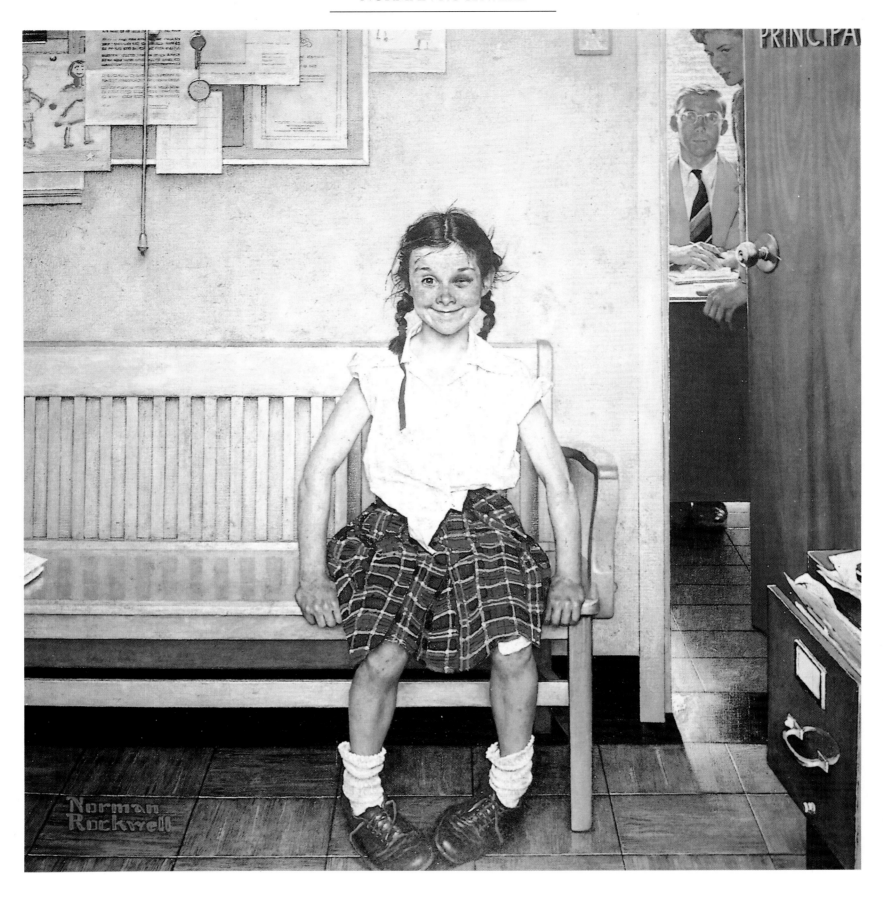

Outside the Principal's Office
Original oil painting for a *Post* cover, 23 May 1953

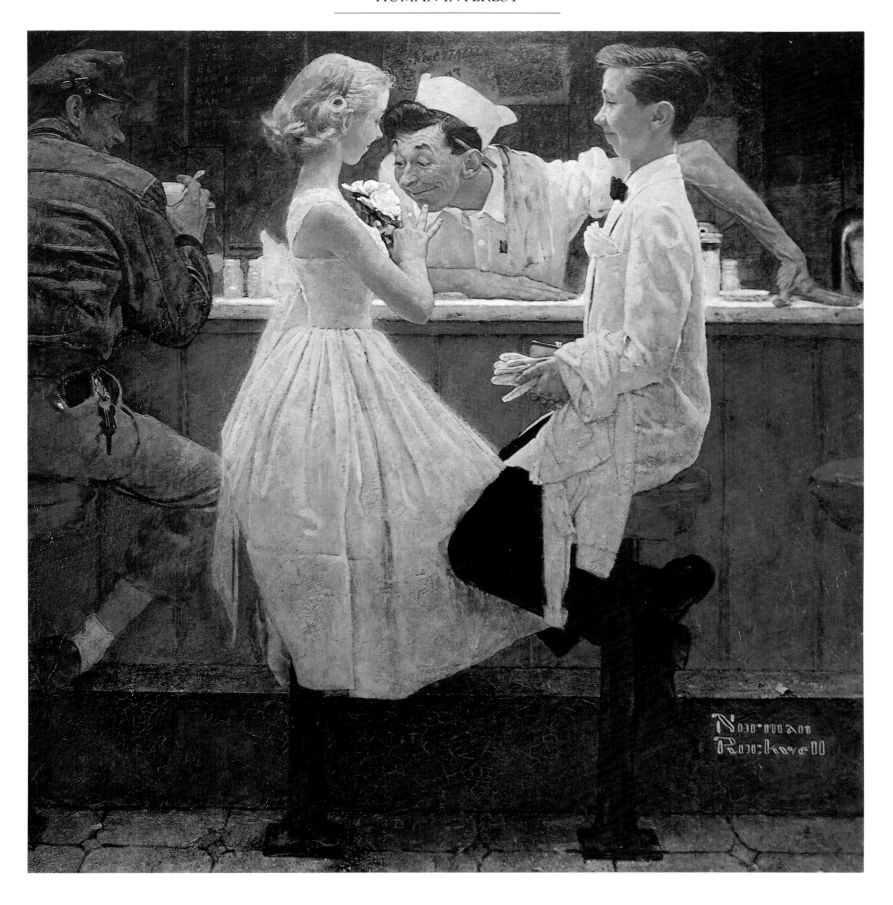

After the Prom
Original oil painting for a *Post* cover, 25 May 1957

PEOPLE AND PLACES

One winter night in 1951, Norman Rockwell sat talking in Arlington, Vermont, with his friends Jack Atherton and George Hughes. As sometimes happened, Rockwell was having trouble with a painting, and he admitted that he had become so frustrated with this particular one that he had pitched it out his studio window into a snow drift. When his friends asked the subject of the painting, Rockwell described it as "an old lady sitting in a railroad diner with a kid and they're praying at the table. A bunch of toughs are looking over at them." Not one to mince words, Hughes looked over at Rockwell and told him that the idea stank.

The next day, Rockwell dusted the snow off the painting and carried it back to his studio for some more work. The finished painting, *Saying Grace*, was one of Rockwell's best and best-loved scenes of everyday people shown in familiar places. As so often with Rockwells, the picture *almost* crosses the line into mere sentimentality, and is saved in large part because it seems to reflect the artist's own sincerity. Rockwell himself admitted that the scene was unlikely and that the onlookers probably would have been a good deal less reverential to an old lady and her grandson saying grace in a roadside diner. Still, he was painting a typical "storytelling picture" which showed life as it *should* be. However idealistic these pictures may appear, Rockwell managed to gain the viewers' acceptance of his vision of American life.

It's not surprising that *Saying Grace* was one of Rockwell's most popular paintings, as it exemplifies all that is best in his genre scenes of everyday life. The picture is painted with the photographic realism which led Rockwell to boast that he'd "always been known as The Kid with the Camera Eye." Needless to say, the seedylooking diner in *Saying Grace* is a real one which Rockwell visited repeatedly in Troy, New York. The table and chairs are ones he'd noticed at an automat in New York City – and had shipped to his Vermont studio. Rockwell's son Jarvis posed as the boy, and the other figures were Arlington locals.

Rockwell's son Peter, himself an artist, said of *Saying Grace*: "My father was very different from most other twentieth-century artists. He was a thinking painter rather than a visual painter. There are no useless details in this painting, and every detail has a design function as well. For example, even the red seats on the chairs have been used to isolate the figures in the center of the composition. Nothing is left to chance."

In *Saying Grace*, as in all his best works, Rockwell brought photographic realism to bear on a mundane subject, and managed to suggest a story beyond the mere moment. Perhaps the old woman and her grandson are traveling cross-country by bus; catching a quick meal in the diner before resuming their trip, they try to make the moment more homey by saying grace over their food.

Saying Grace was Rockwell's most popular *Post* cover, bringing in as much fan mail as *The Four Freedoms*. The popularity of this single cover was rivaled only by the famous *Post* series of feature paintings known as "Norman Rockwell Visits . . ." Throughout the series, as in all Rockwell's best work, his particular ability to show real people in a familiar setting shines through. Nostalgia never obscured his eye for detail, although it informed his view of American people and places.

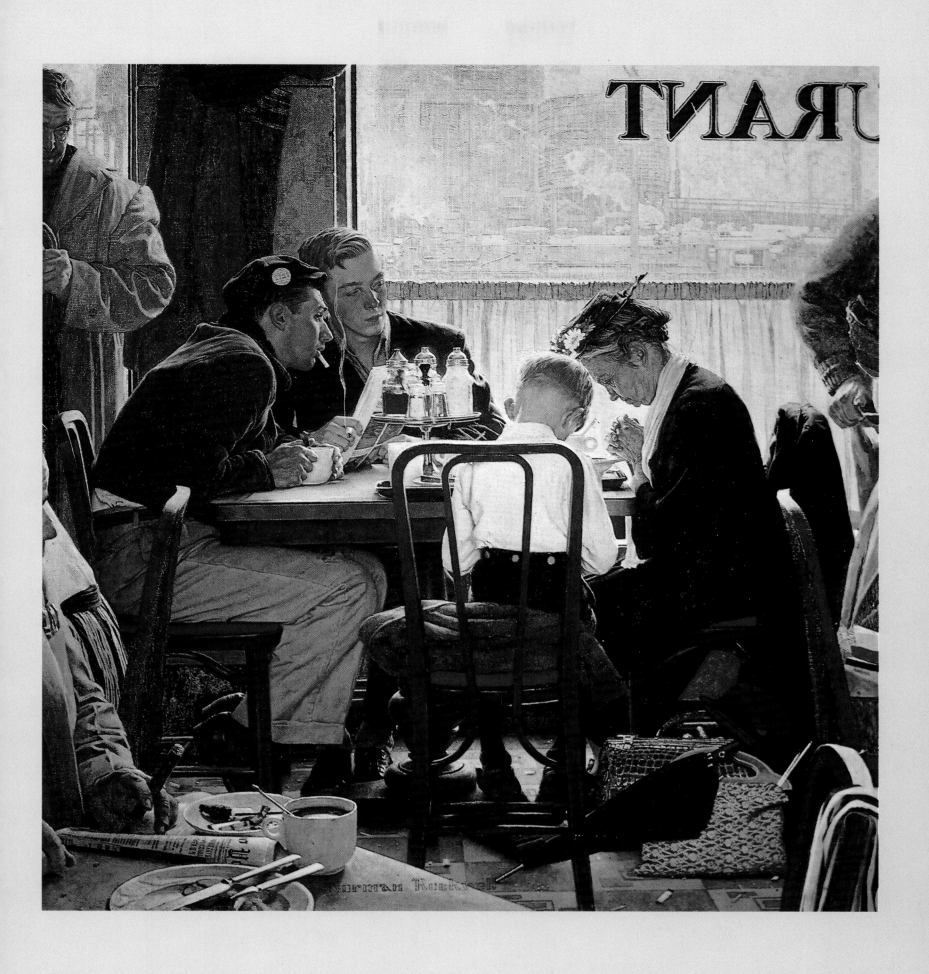

Saying Grace
Post cover, 24 November 1951

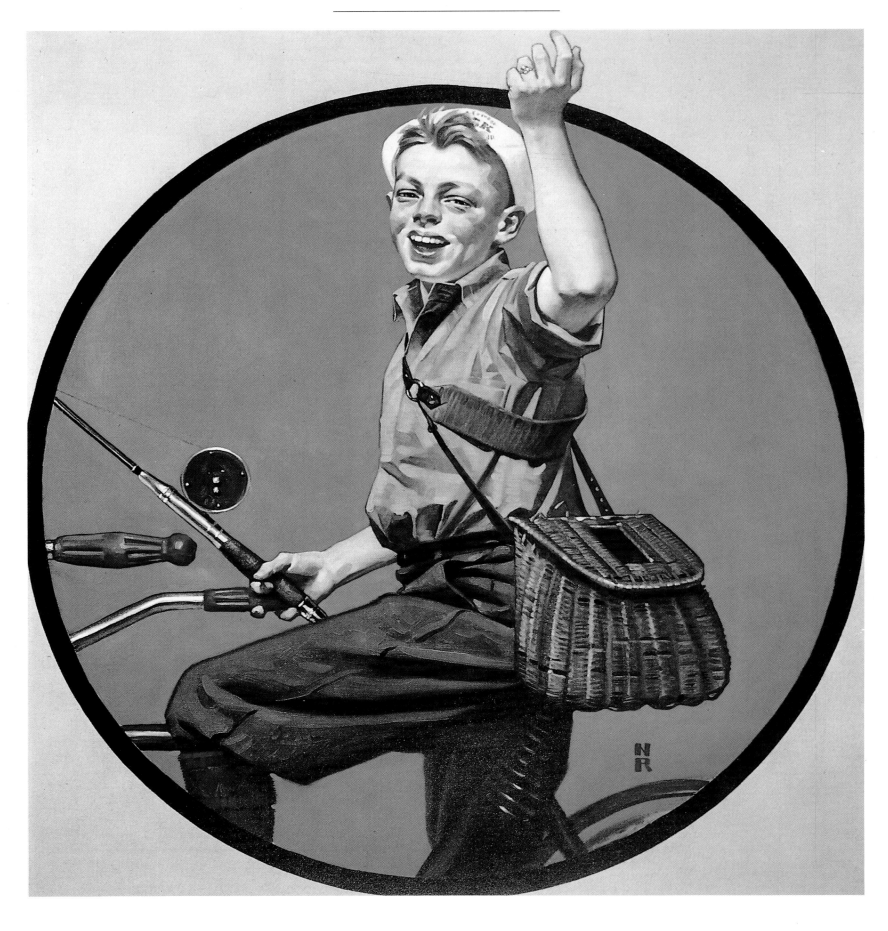

Off to Fish on a Bike
Advertisement for Fisk bicycle tires *Boy's Life*,
September 1919

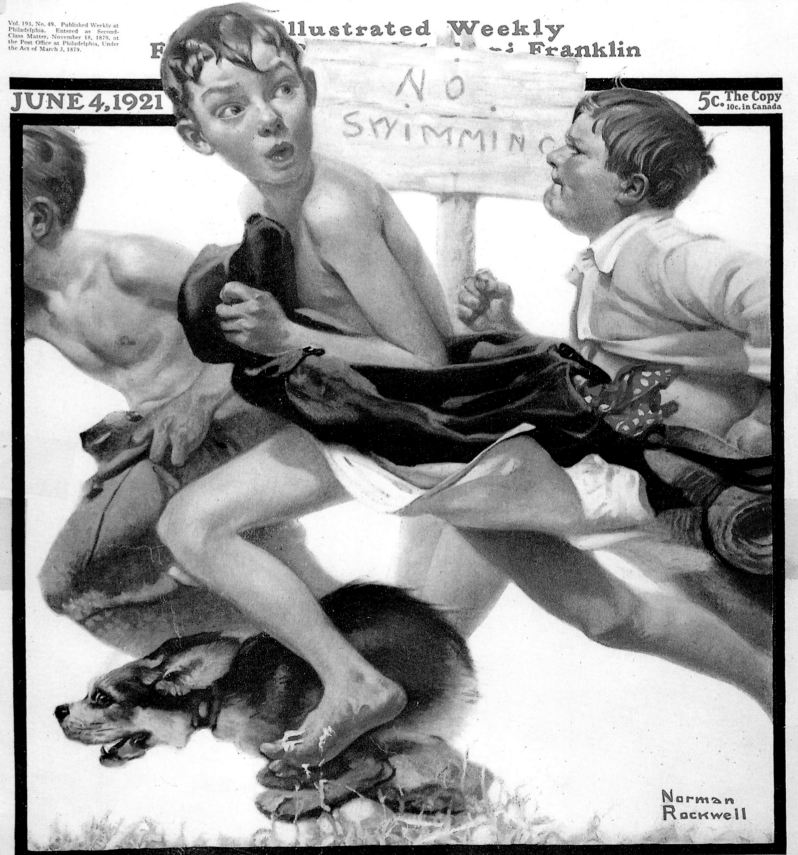

No Swimming
Post cover, 4 June 1921

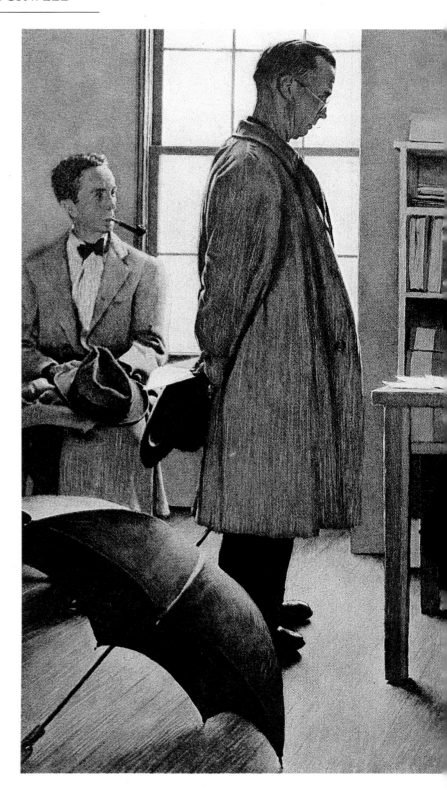

Norman Rockwell Visits a Ration Board
Post illustration, 15 July 1944

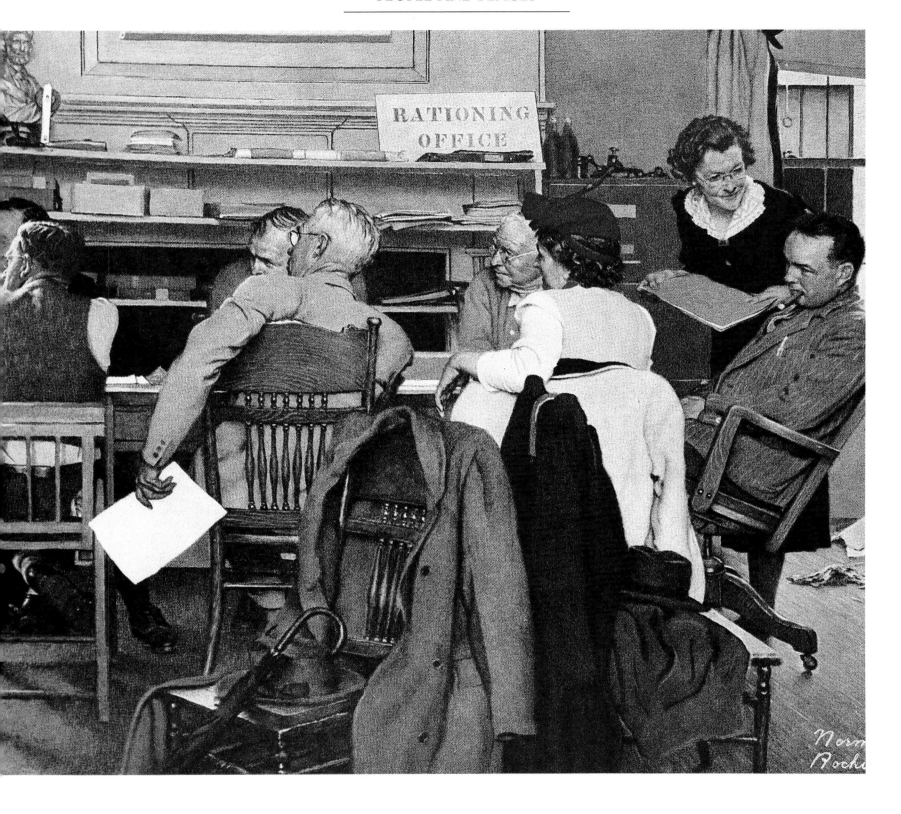

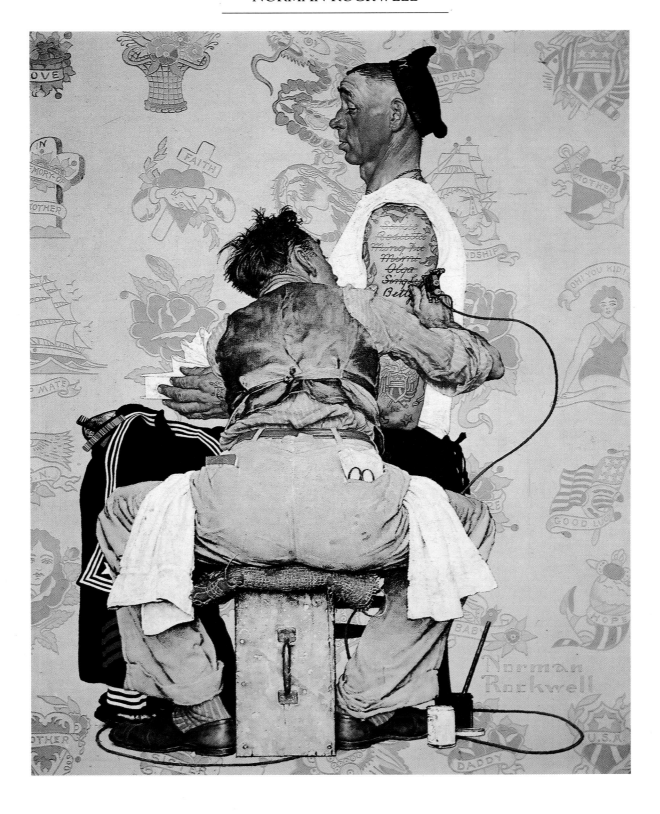

The Tattooist
Original oil painting for a *Post* cover, 4 March 1944

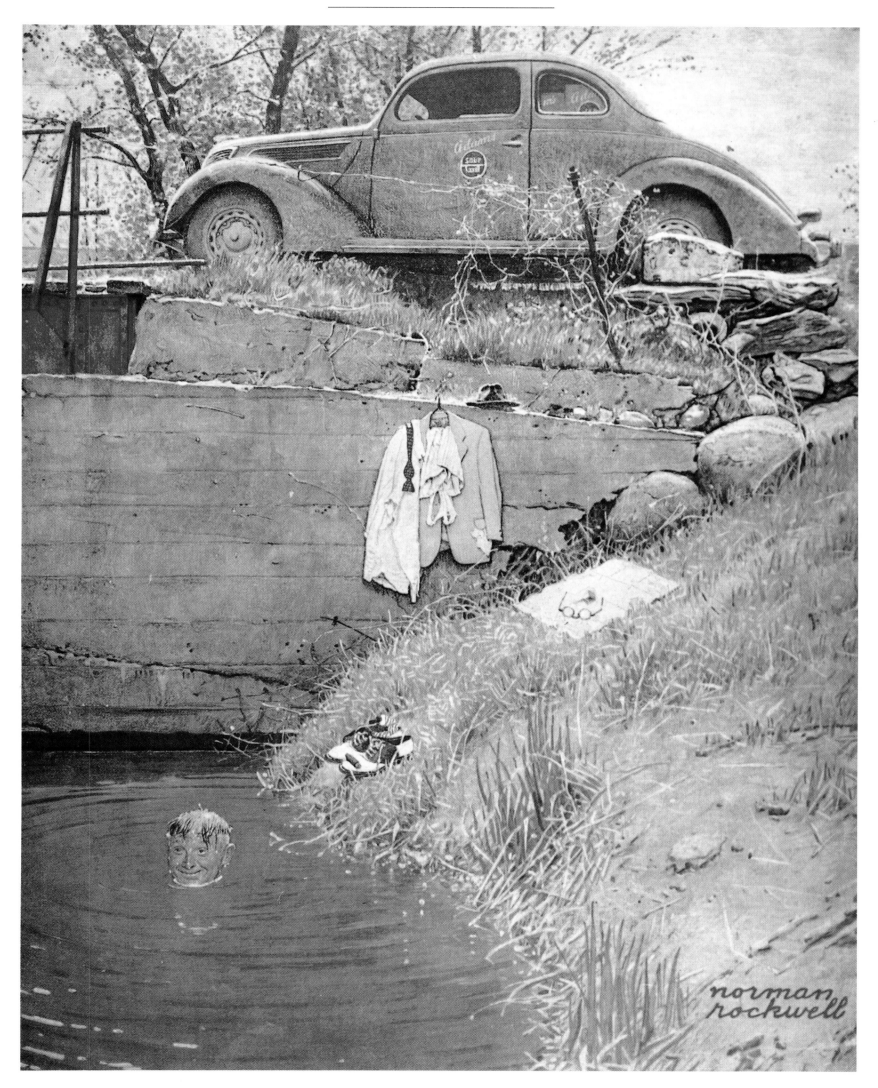

The Swimming Hole
Original oil painting for a *Post* cover, 11 August 1945

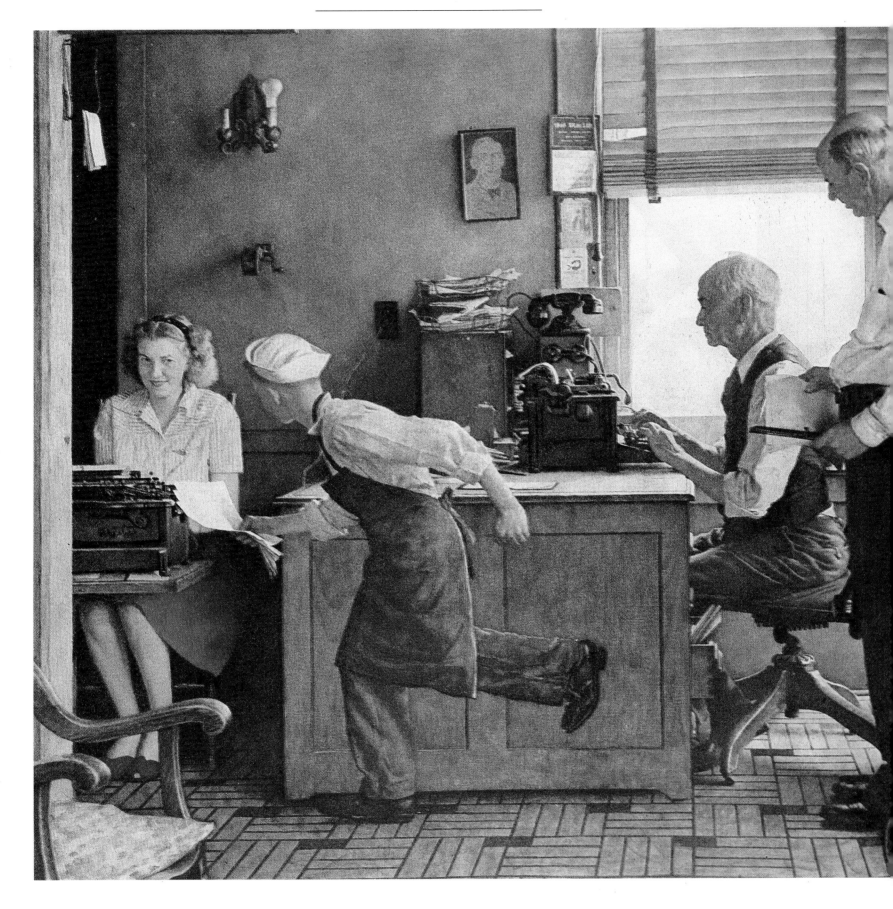

Norman Rockwell Visits a Country Editor
Post illustration, 25 May 1946

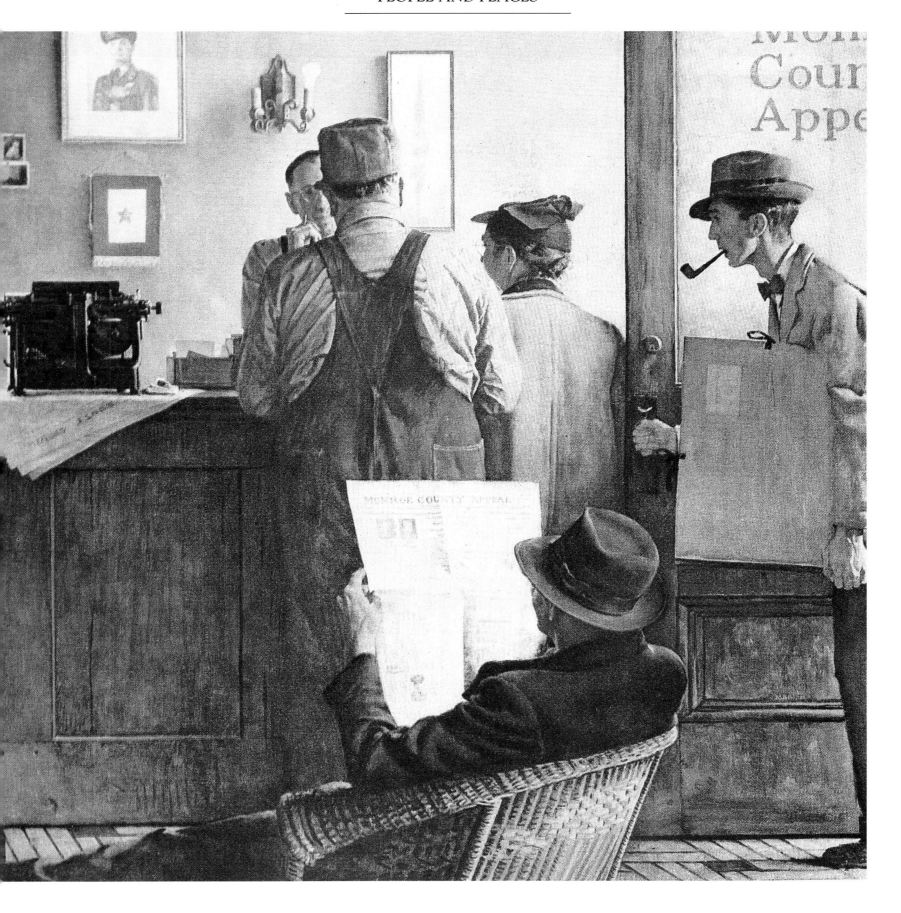

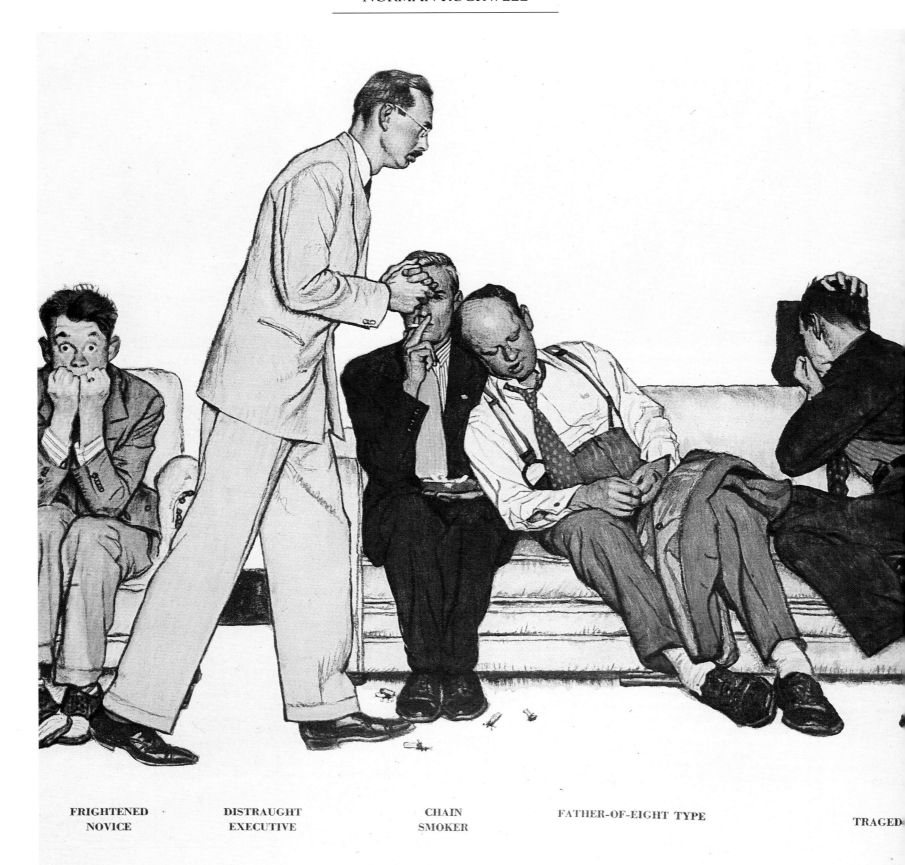

FRIGHTENED
NOVICE

DISTRAUGHT
EXECUTIVE

CHAIN
SMOKER

FATHER-OF-EIGHT TYPE

TRAGED

Maternity Waiting Room
Post illustration, 13 July 1946

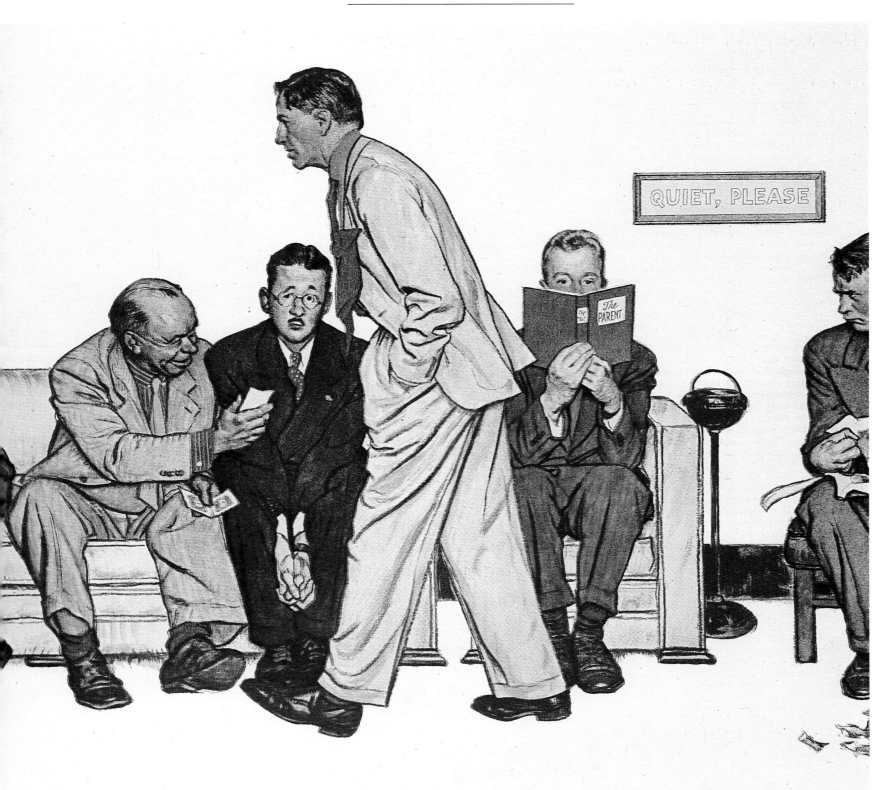

HEARTY-SALESMAN
TYPE

BELIEVER IN
THE WORST

PACER

THE EARNEST-
PARENT TYPE

MAGAZINE
SHREDDER

13

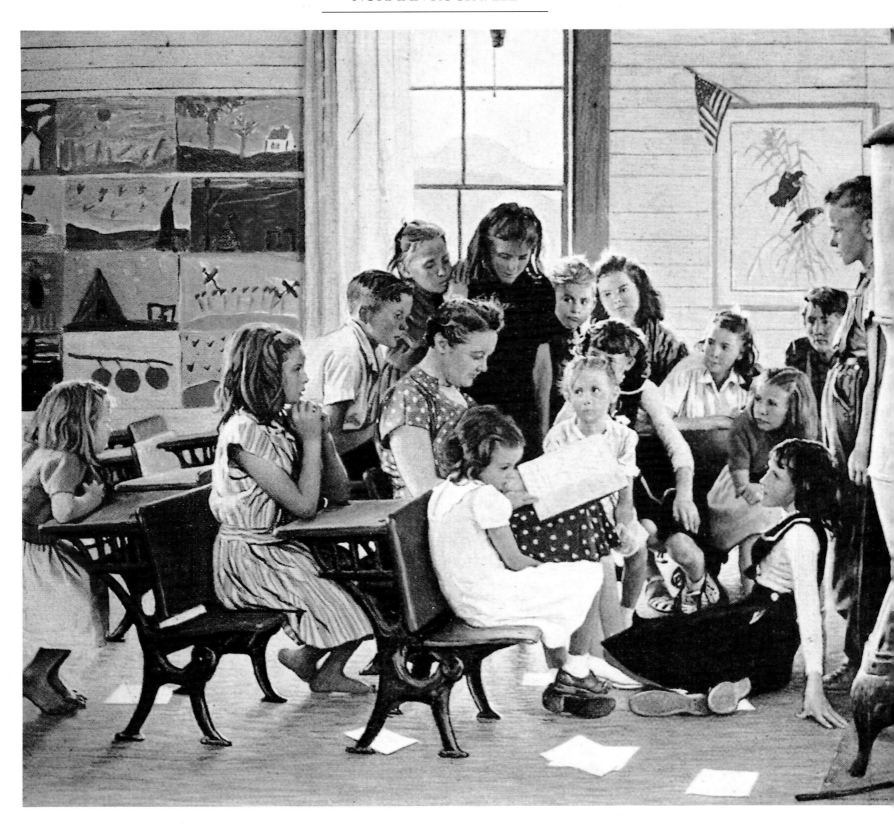

Norman Rockwell Visits a Country School
Post illustration, 2 November 1946

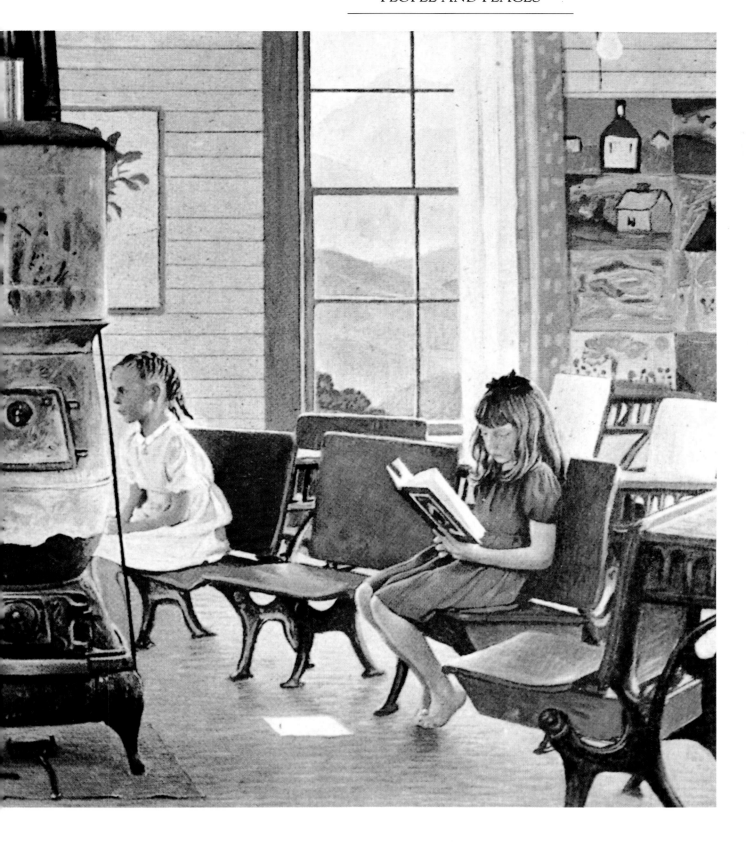

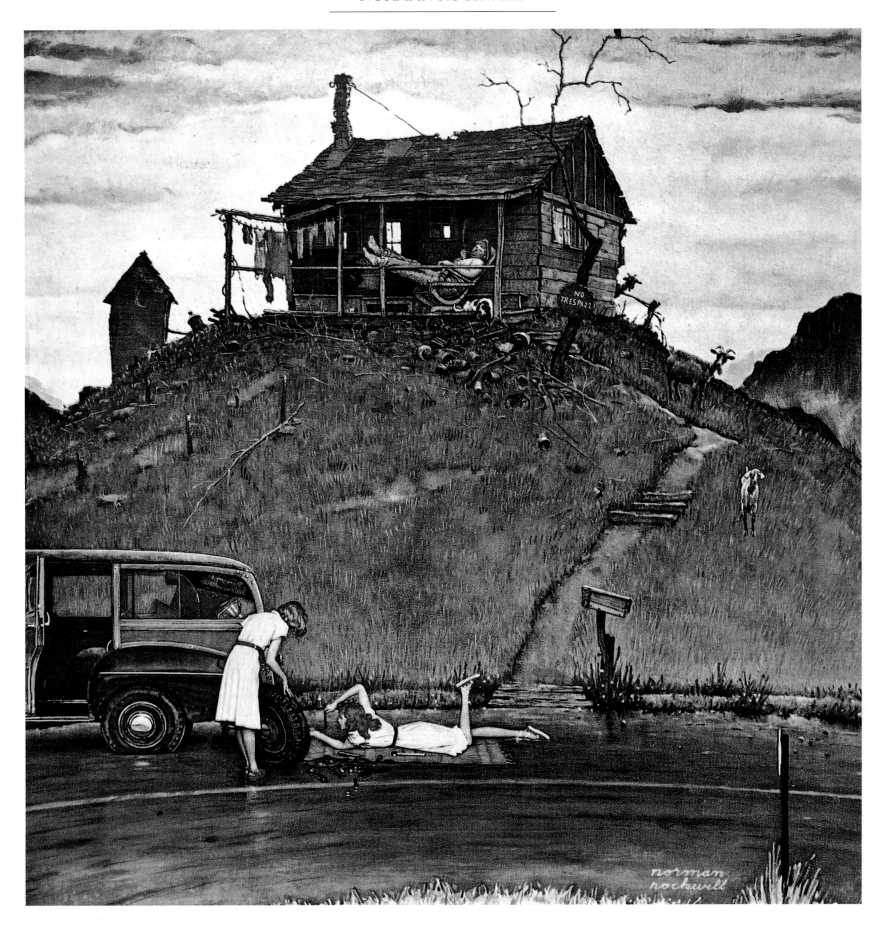

Fixing a Flat
Post cover, 3 August 1946

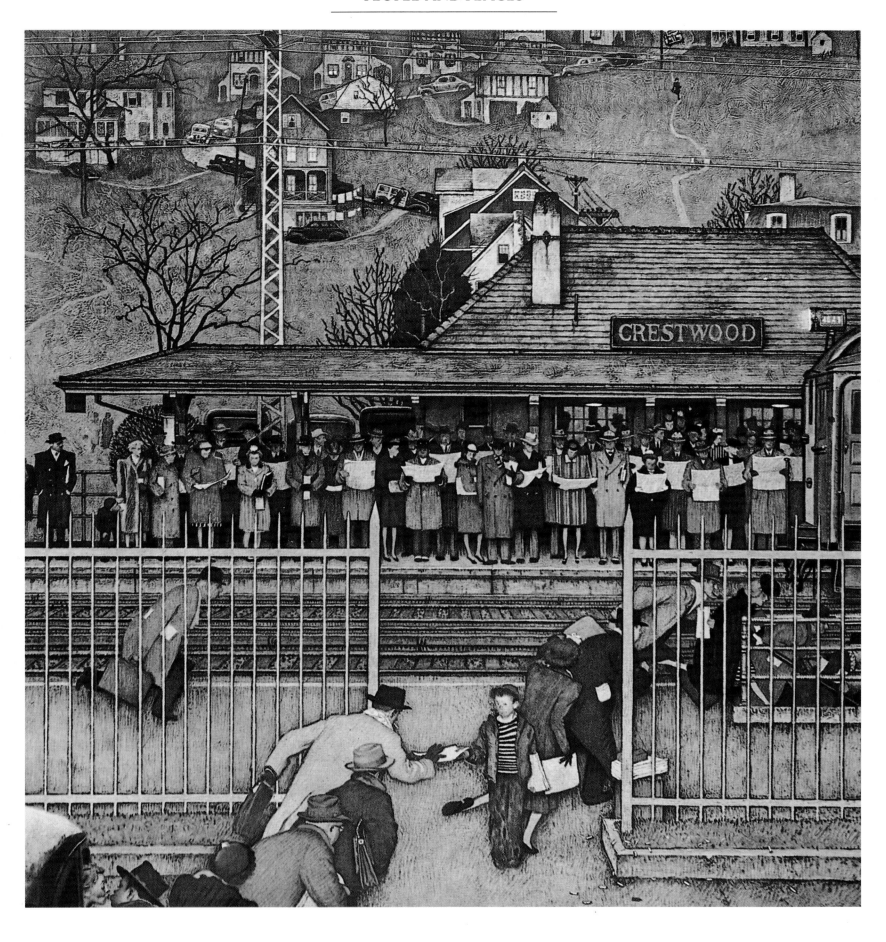

Commuters
Post cover, 16 November 1946

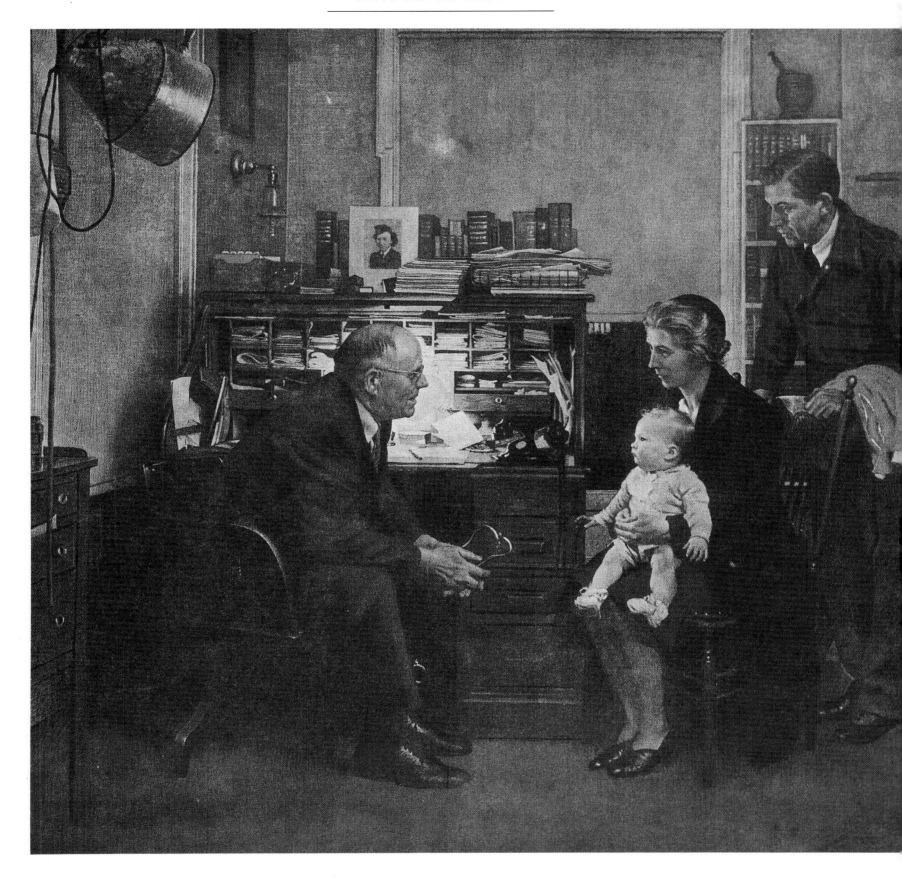

Norman Rockwell Visits a Country Doctor
Post illustration, 12 April 1947

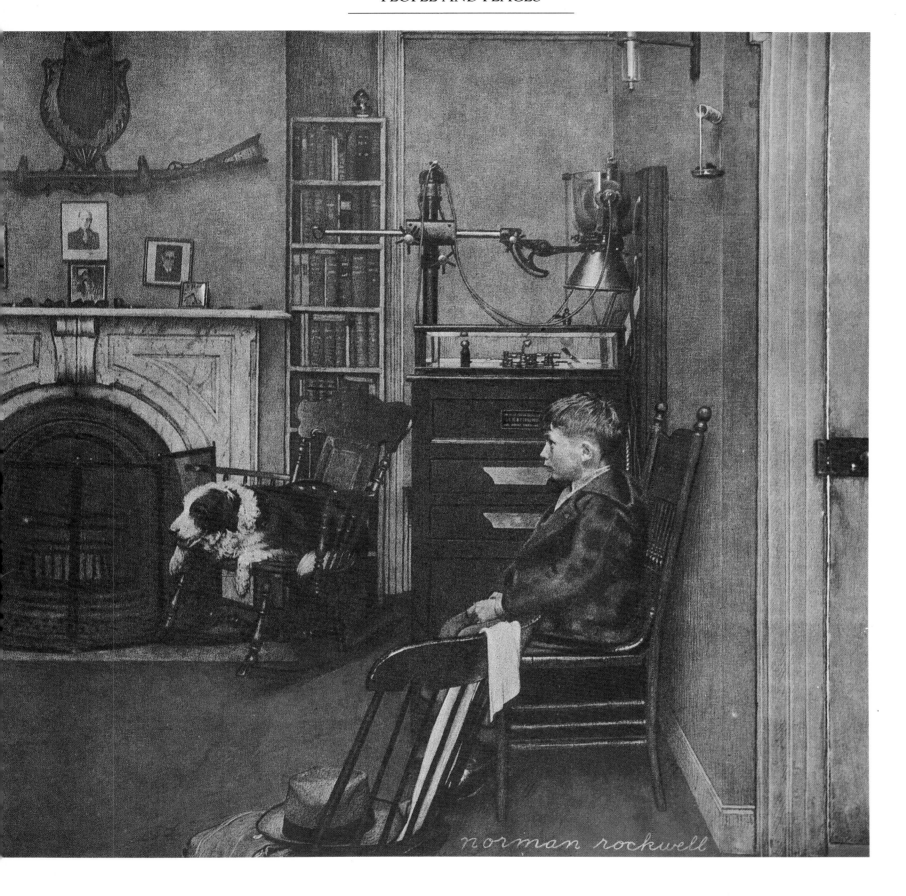

norman rockwell

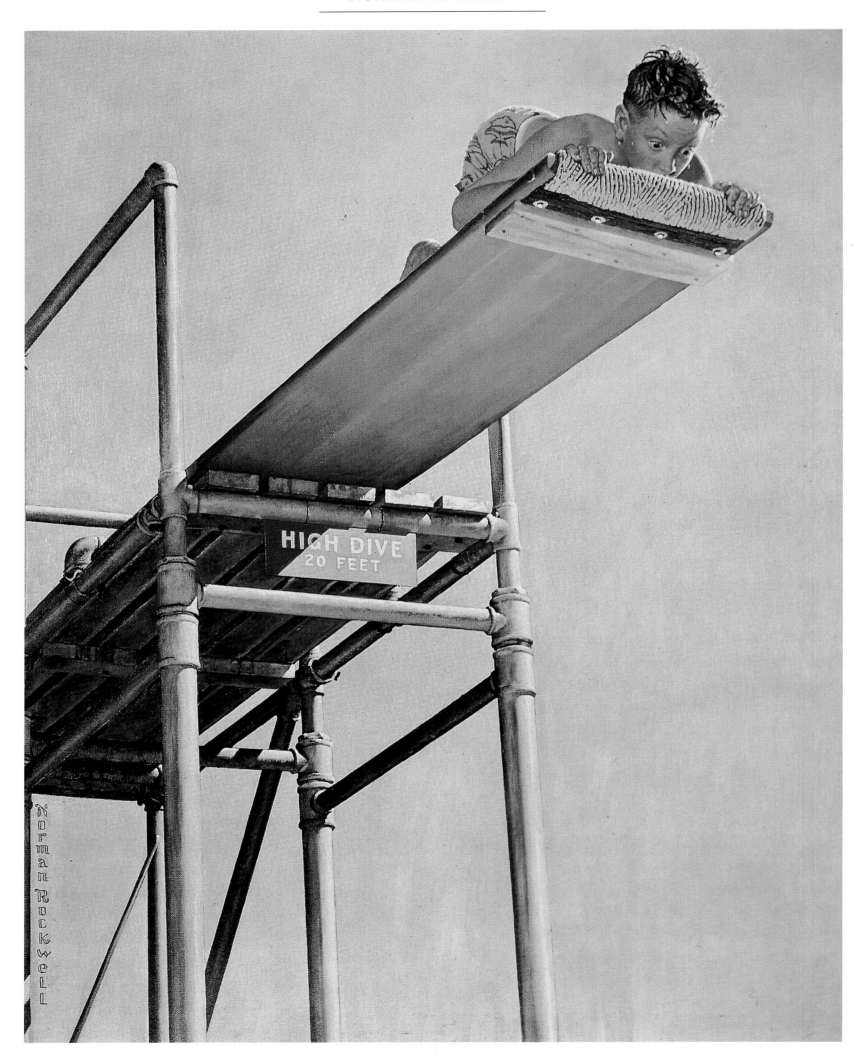

The Diving Board
Original oil painting for a *Post* cover, 16 August 1947

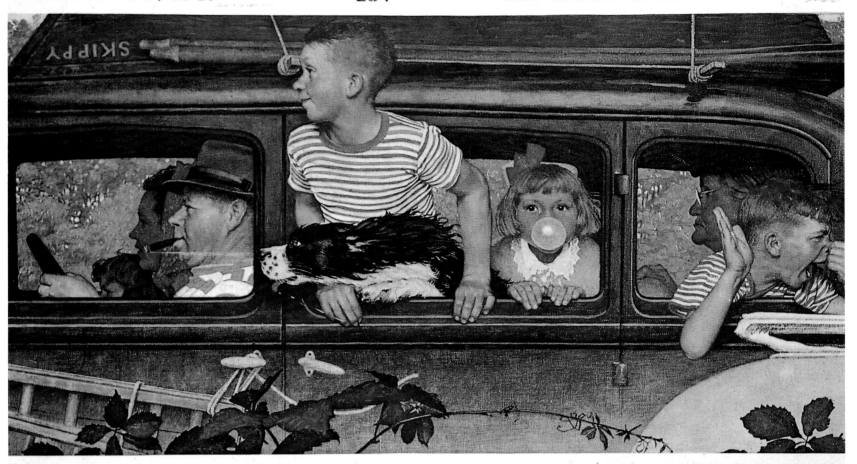

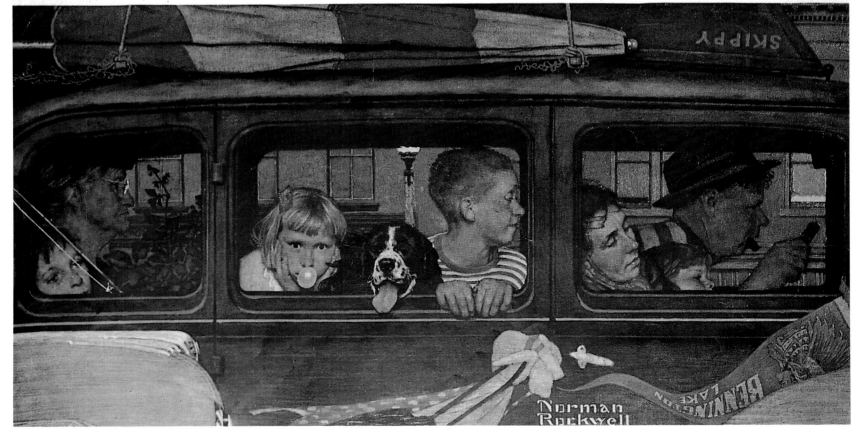

The Outing
Post cover, 30 August 1947

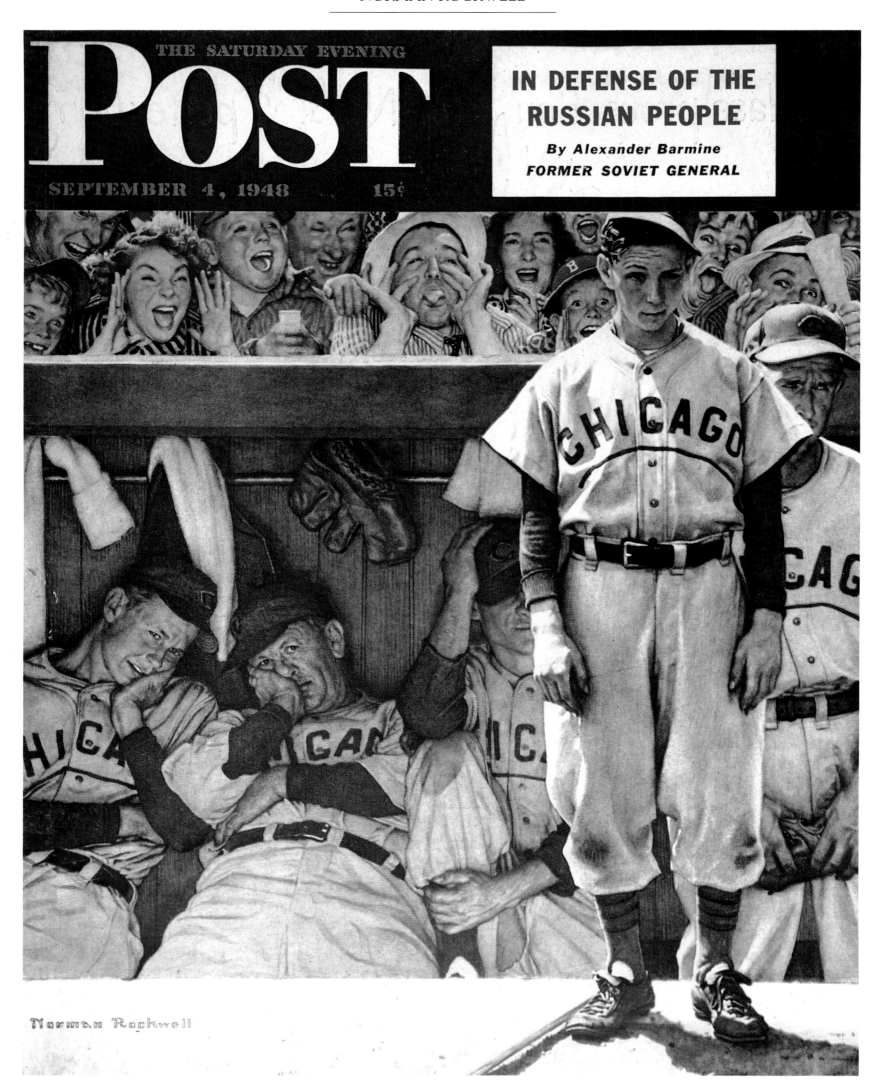

The Dugout
Post cover, 4 September 1948

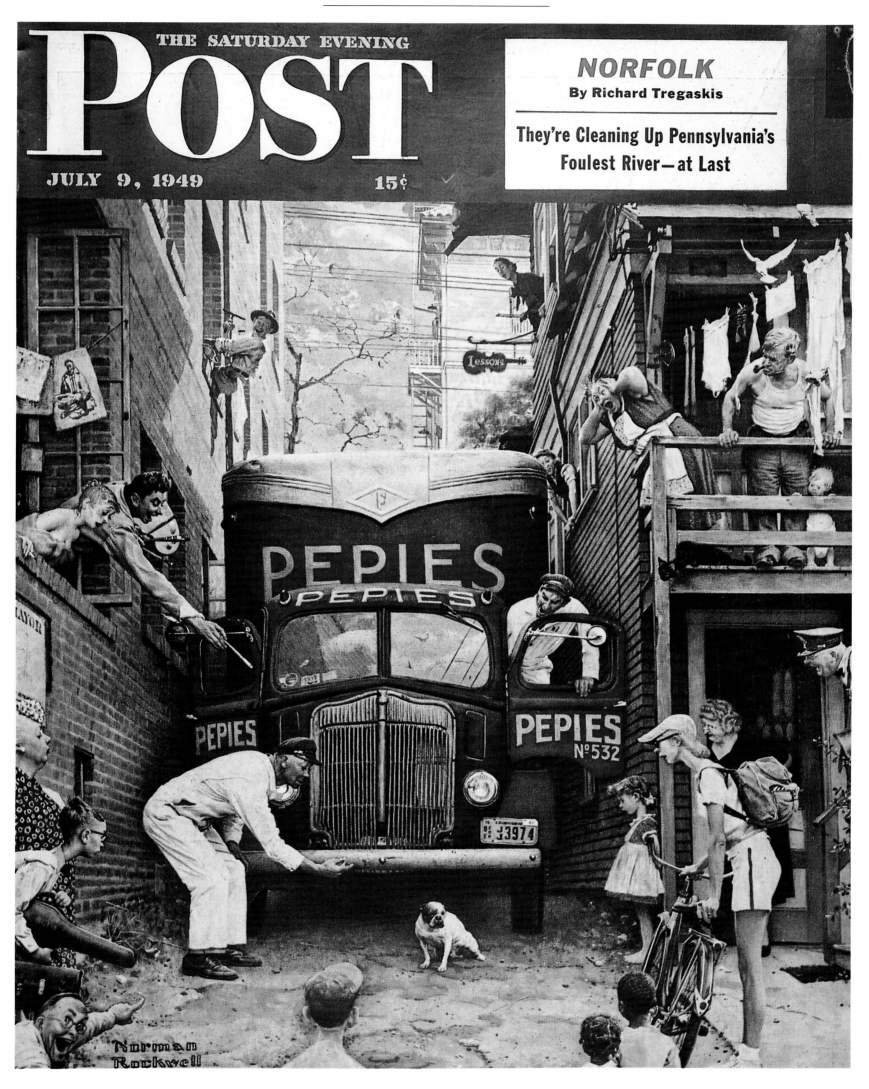

Traffic Conditions
Post cover, 9 July 1949

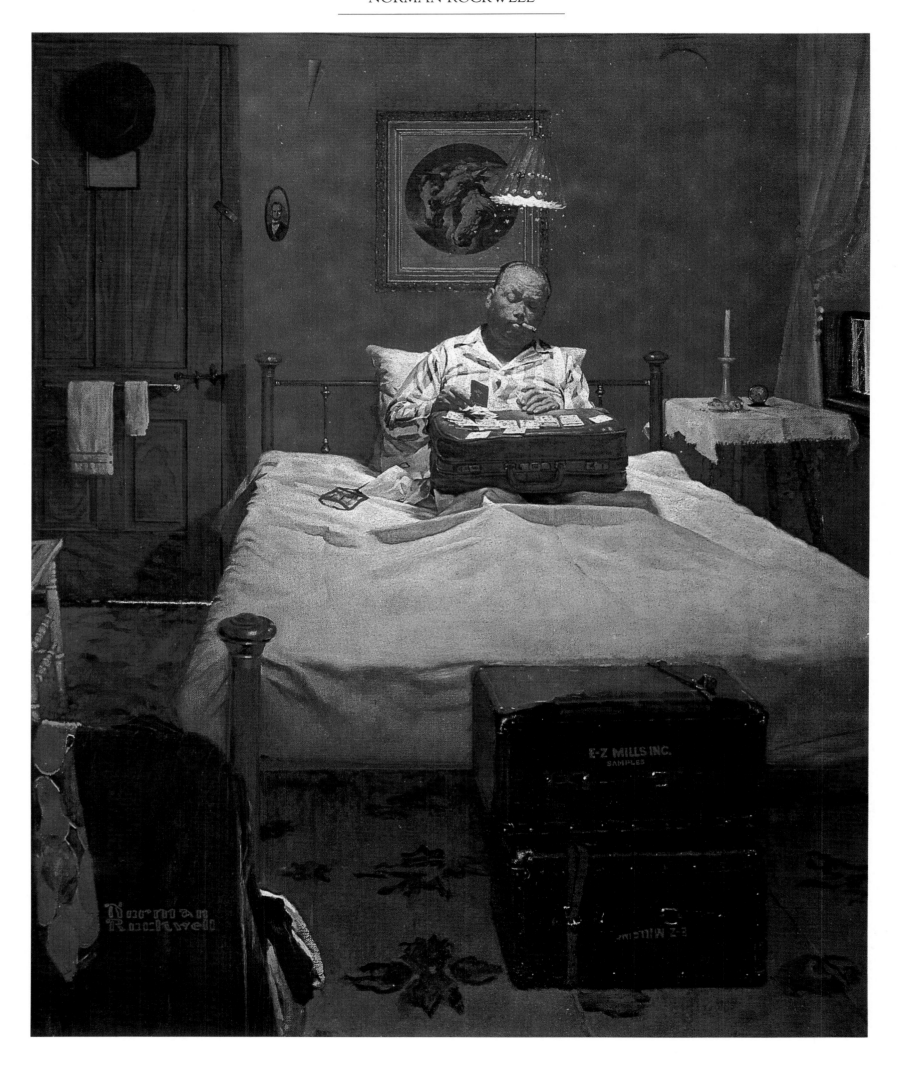

Solitaire
Post cover, 19 August 1950

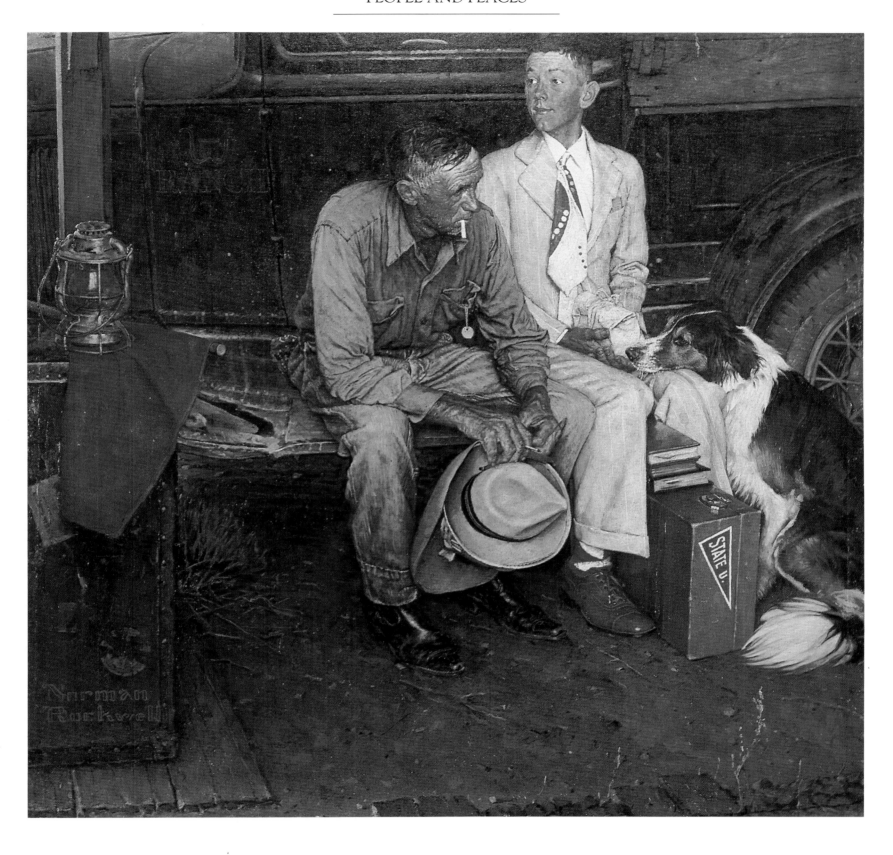

Breaking Home Ties
Original oil painting for a *Post* cover, 25 September 1954. Collection Don Trachte

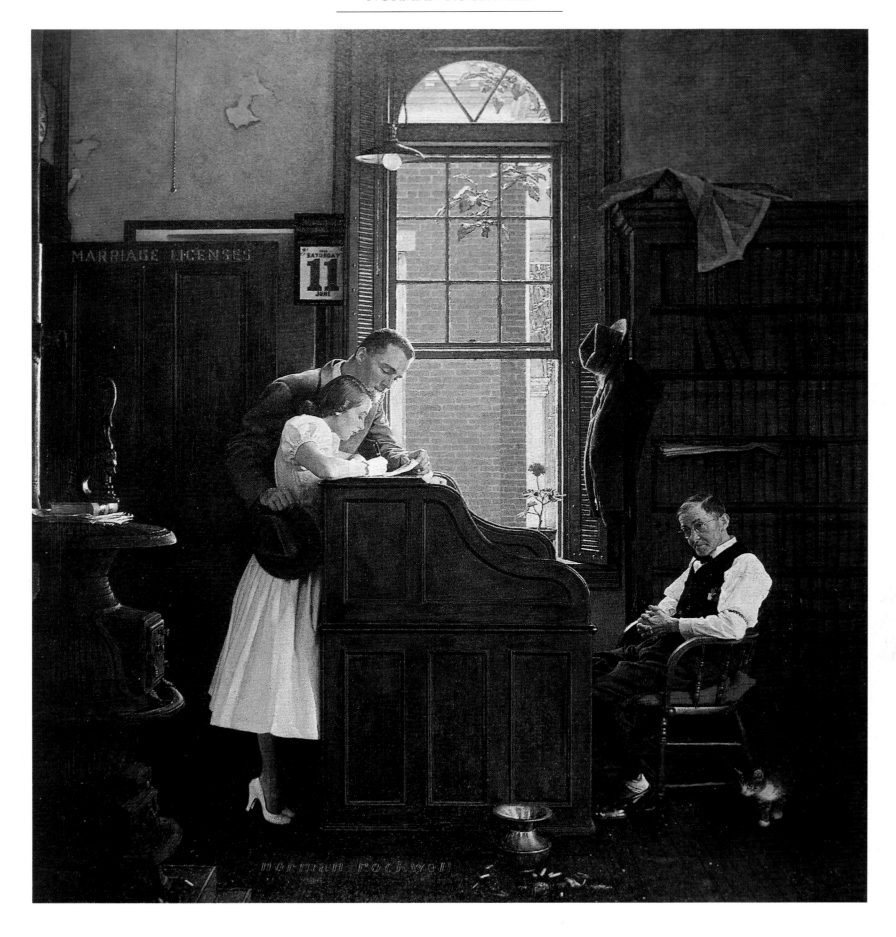

The Marriage License
Original oil painting for a *Post* cover, 11 June 1955

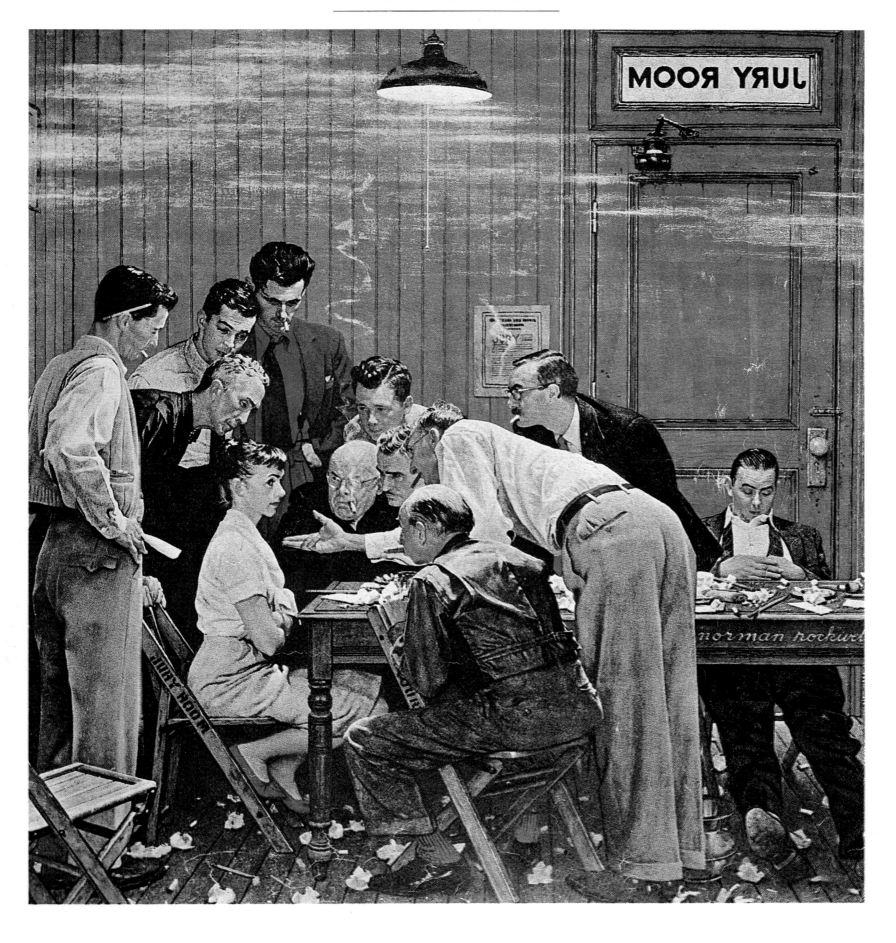

The Jury
Post cover, 14 February 1959

Pages 66-67:
New Kids in the Neighborhood
Look illustration, 16 May 1967

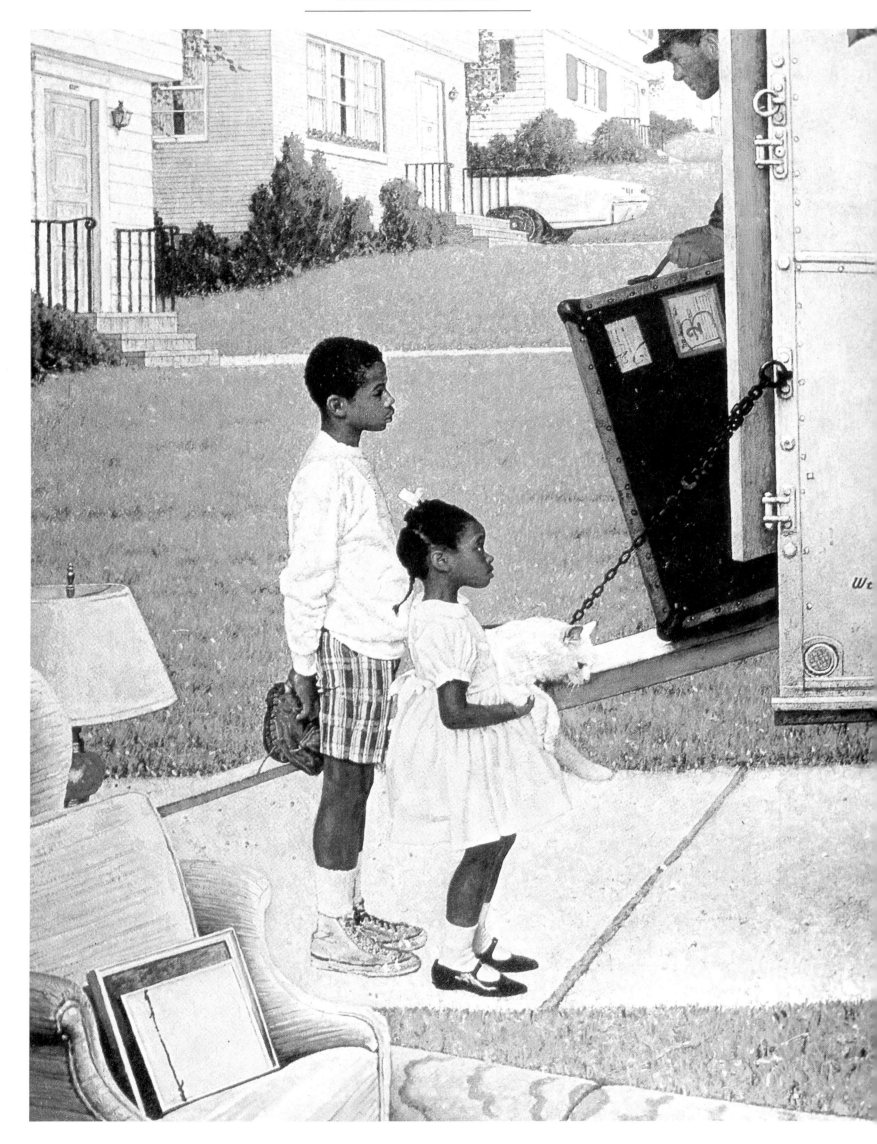

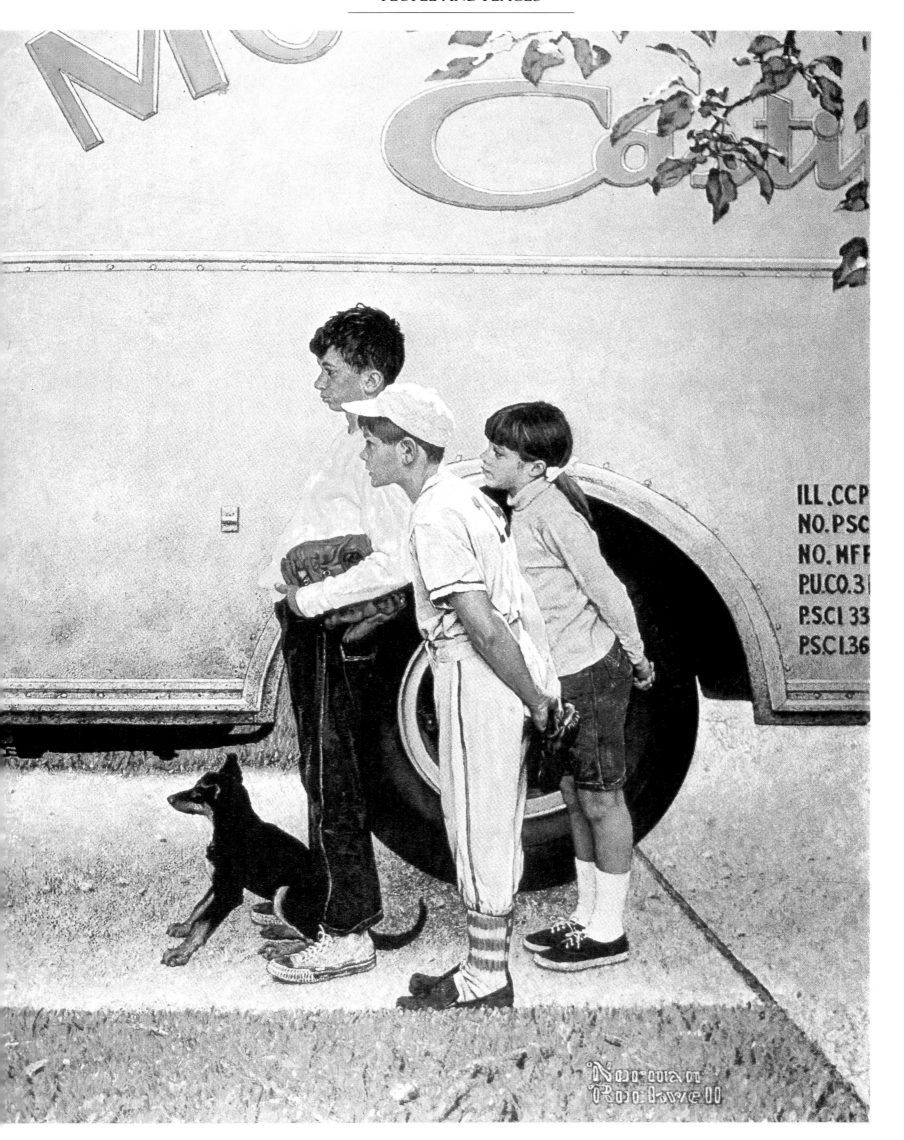

HISTORY AND HOLIDAYS

From the 1920s through the 1960s, Norman Rockwell holiday covers were a *Saturday Evening Post* tradition. Rockwell Santas were shown coming down chimneys, riding on subways, making up lists and checking them twice, falling asleep over unfinished toys while their elfin helpers worked on through the night; in fact, over the years, Rockwell showed Santas in almost every imaginable way to provide fresh holiday scenes for the *Post*. He also did numerous Christmas cards for Hallmark Cards, as well as holiday scenes for calendars. Rockwell always wanted his work to have the widest possible audience; he would have been delighted at today's flourishing market in Rockwell commemorative figurines and collector's plates.

As the years passed, it wasn't always easy for Rockwell to come up with a new holiday idea. One of the most popular *Post* holiday covers, the 1945 *Home for Thanksgiving* was even more problematic than *Saying Grace*. Rockwell began thinking about the Thanksgiving cover in August and hit on the idea of showing a serviceman home for the holidays, sitting in the family kitchen while his mother put the finishing touches on the Thanksgiving dinner. Rockwell had his basic idea, but was still having trouble visualizing just what he wanted to show. As often, when he had difficulty coming up with a good idea, Rockwell decided that he needed a change of scene. Along with his good friend Arthur Guptill, who later wrote *Norman Rockwell, Illustrator*, Rockwell headed north into Maine where he hoped to visit Winslow Homer's studio outside Portland and find the perfect spot for a *Post* Thanksgiving cover set in a rural kitchen.

A Maine friend of Guptill's steered Rockwell to just the house he needed: an 1834 shipbuilder's cottage in Pennellville. The kitchen, with its old-fashioned wood stove, seemed perfect – but Rockwell still had to find his models. Rockwell and Guptill drove off to Brunswick, where the local USO produced a number of G.I.s for Rockwell to chose from. Somehow, none of them seemed to have just the right face, and Rockwell headed back for Pennellville, where he decided to use a local young man for his G.I.

For the next few days, Rockwell staged the scene he wanted in the Pennellville kitchen. He cajoled a local photographer into photographing the models and kitchen from every angle, so that he could do the final painting from the photos back at his studio in Arlington, Vermont. The local models threw themselves wholeheartedly into posing for the famous artist, with the woman, who played the mother, even whipping up a pie, biscuits, and finally, the turkey itself.

Back in Arlington, Rockwell began work on the cover with his sketches and photographs. Almost immediately, he decided that the young man who had posed as the G.I. was *too* young to make a convincing soldier. Nor was Rockwell sure that the "mother" looked motherly enough. For weeks, Rockwell wrestled with the assignment, and finally came up with a finished painting. The next day, just as Rockwell was about to send his picture off to the *Post*, he decided it wouldn't do; he re-did the entire composition and rushed out a completely new scene, using local models. The finished cover arrived at the *Post* still wet; not many *Post* subscribers could have guessed that the 1945 Thanksgiving cover had taken Rockwell from mid-August almost to Thanksgiving to complete.

During World War II, Rockwell turned out a number of *Post* covers showing G.I.s (especially the famous Willie Gillis series) and created his famous figure of *Rosie the Riveter*, whose pose was based on Michelangelo's *Prophet Isaiah*. Characteristically, Rockwell's portraits of America at war emphasized the home front. He did not go in for combat scenes, but showed reassuring images such as *America at the Polls*, which emphasized what America was fighting to preserve. When the war was over, Rockwell returned to doing what he did best, showing vignettes of American life. One of his last major series of works for *Look* showed America's conquest of outer space. From *Ben Franklin Signing the Declaration of Independence* to *Astronauts on the Moon*, Rockwell recorded the nation's history, just as he commemorated its holidays.

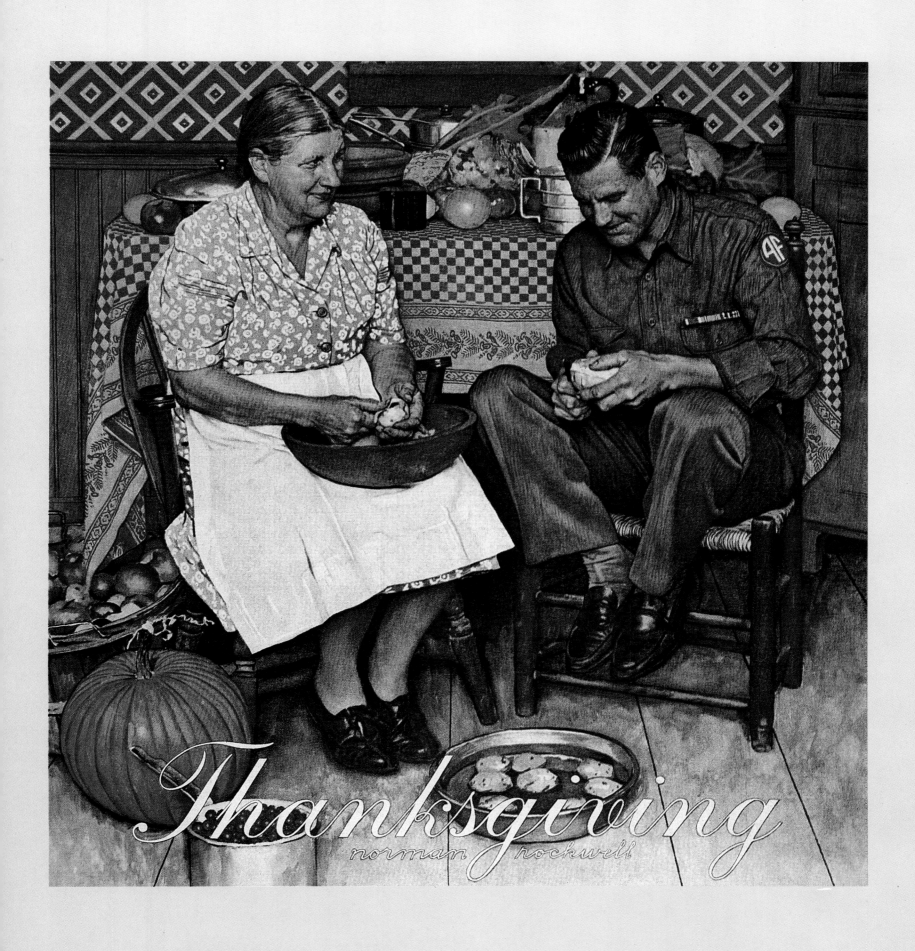

Home for Thanksgiving
Post cover, 24 November 1945

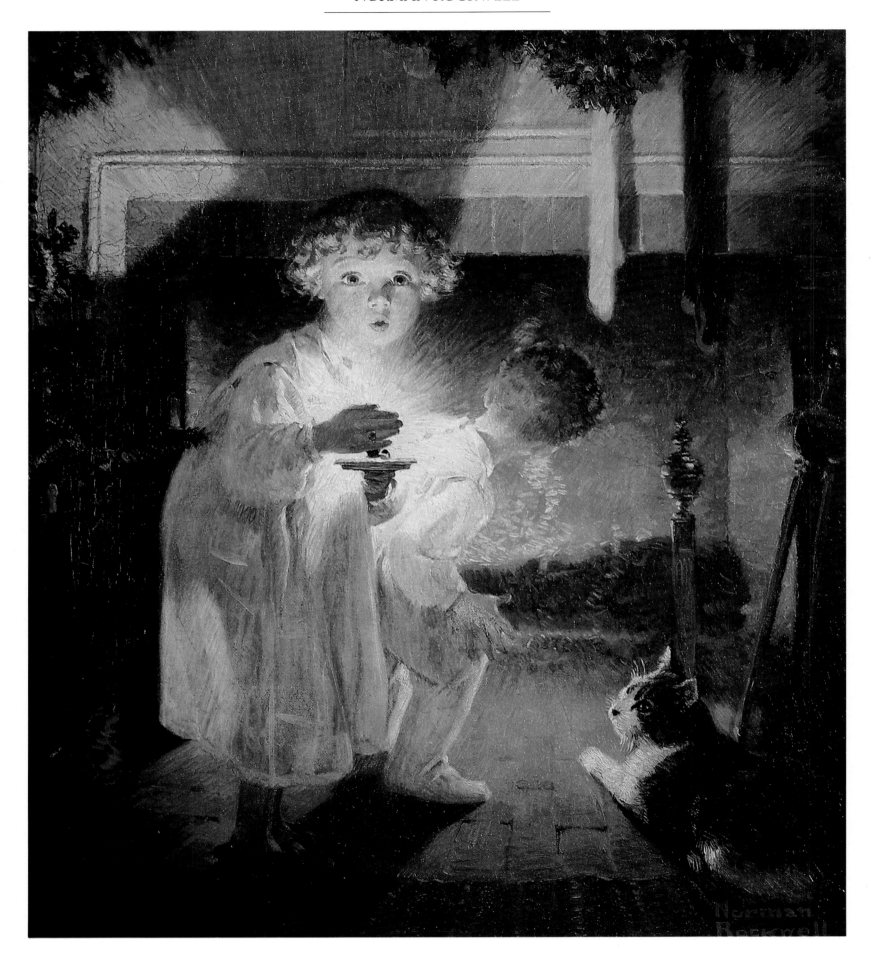

Is He Coming?
Life cover, 16 December 1920

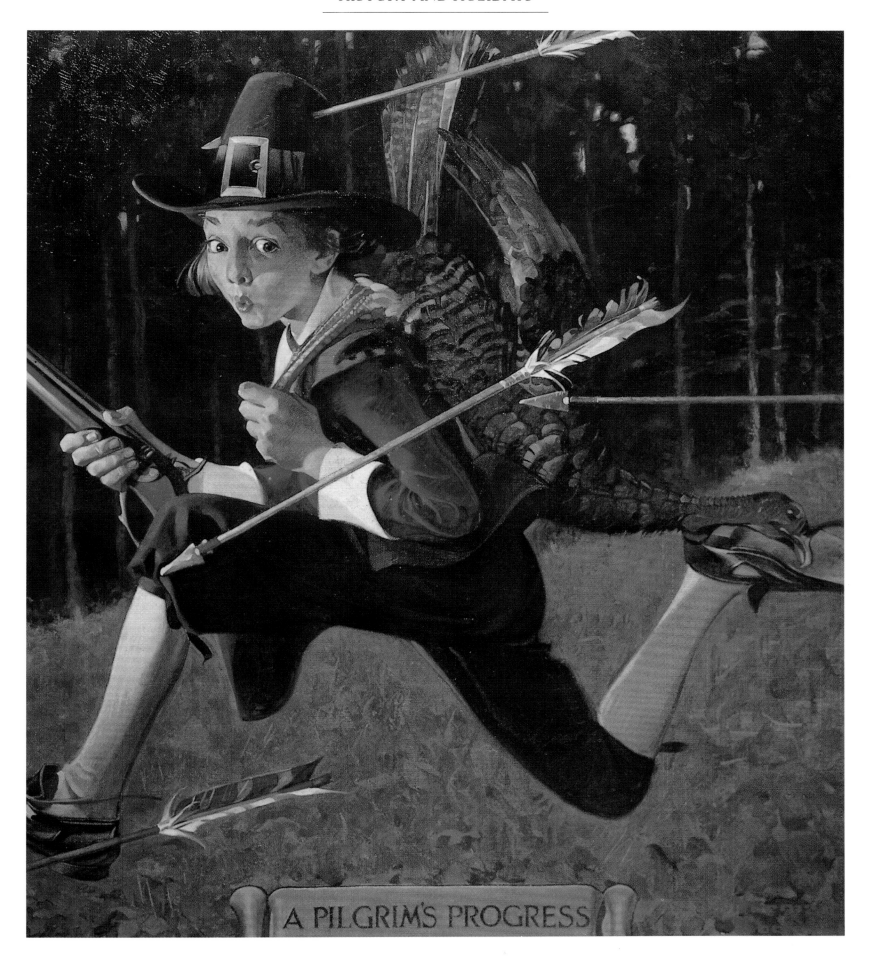

A Pilgrim's Progress
Life cover, 17 November 1921

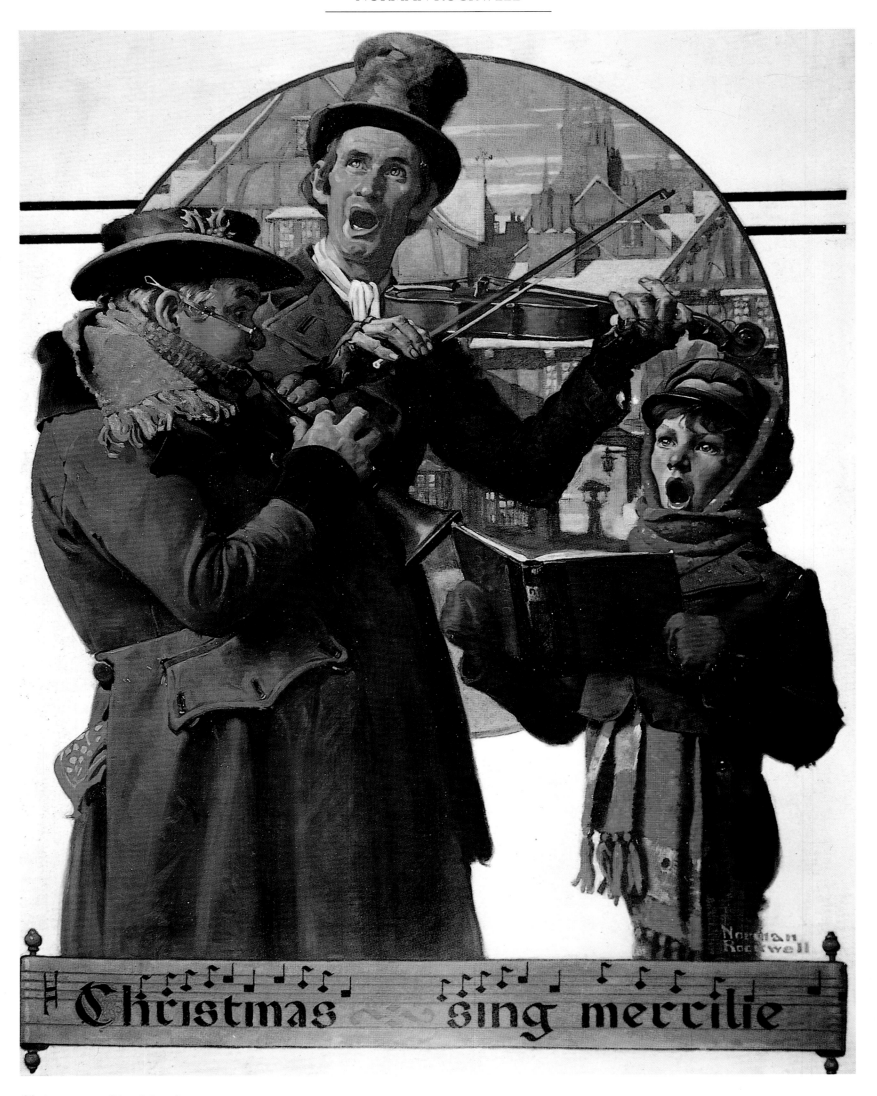

Christmas . . . Sing Merrilie
Original oil painting for a *Post* cover, 8 December 1923

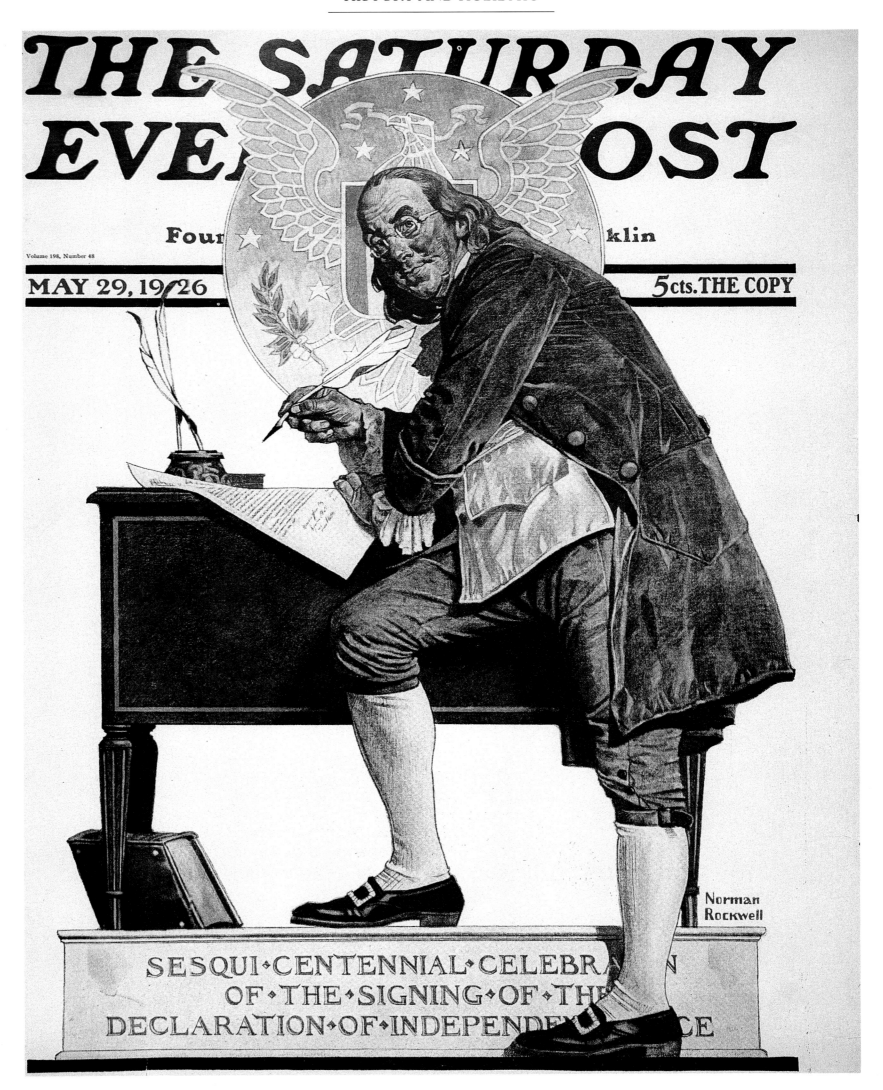

Ben Franklin Signing the Declaration of Independence
Post cover, 29 May 1926

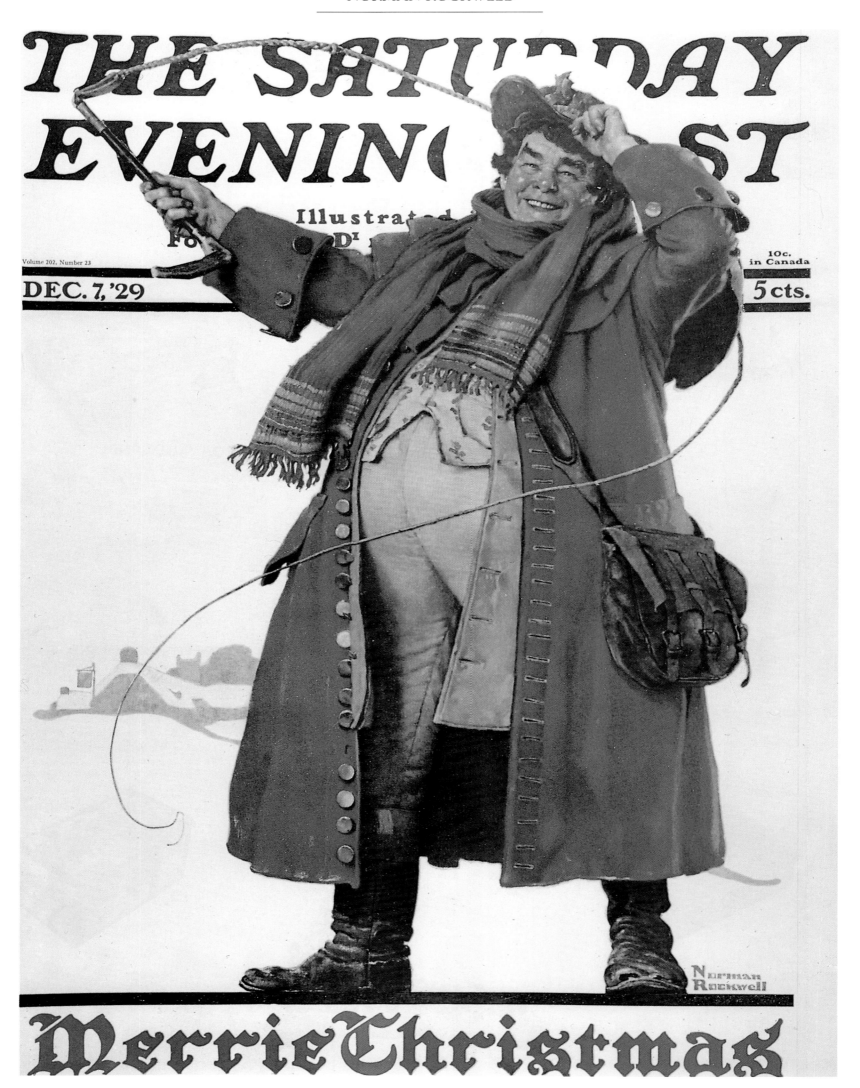

Merrie Christmas
Post cover, 7 December 1929

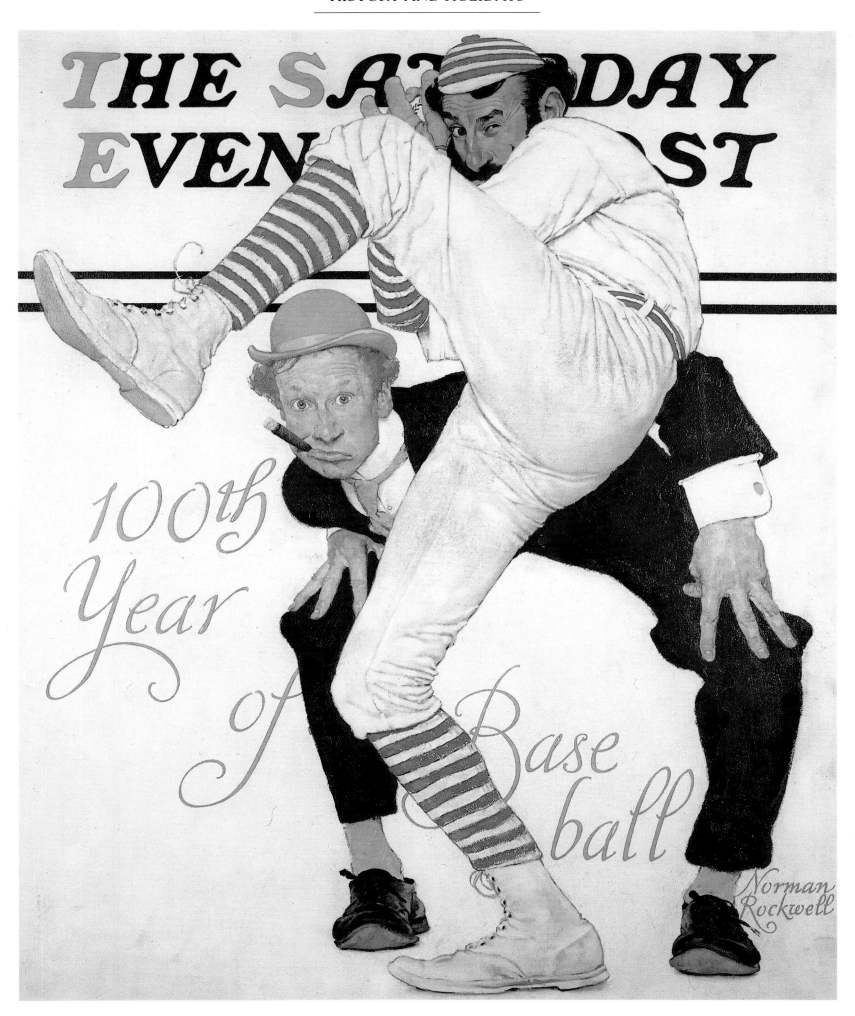

100th Year of Baseball
Original oil painting for a *Post* cover, 8 July 1939
Collection The National Baseball Hall of Fame
and Museum, Cooperstown, NY

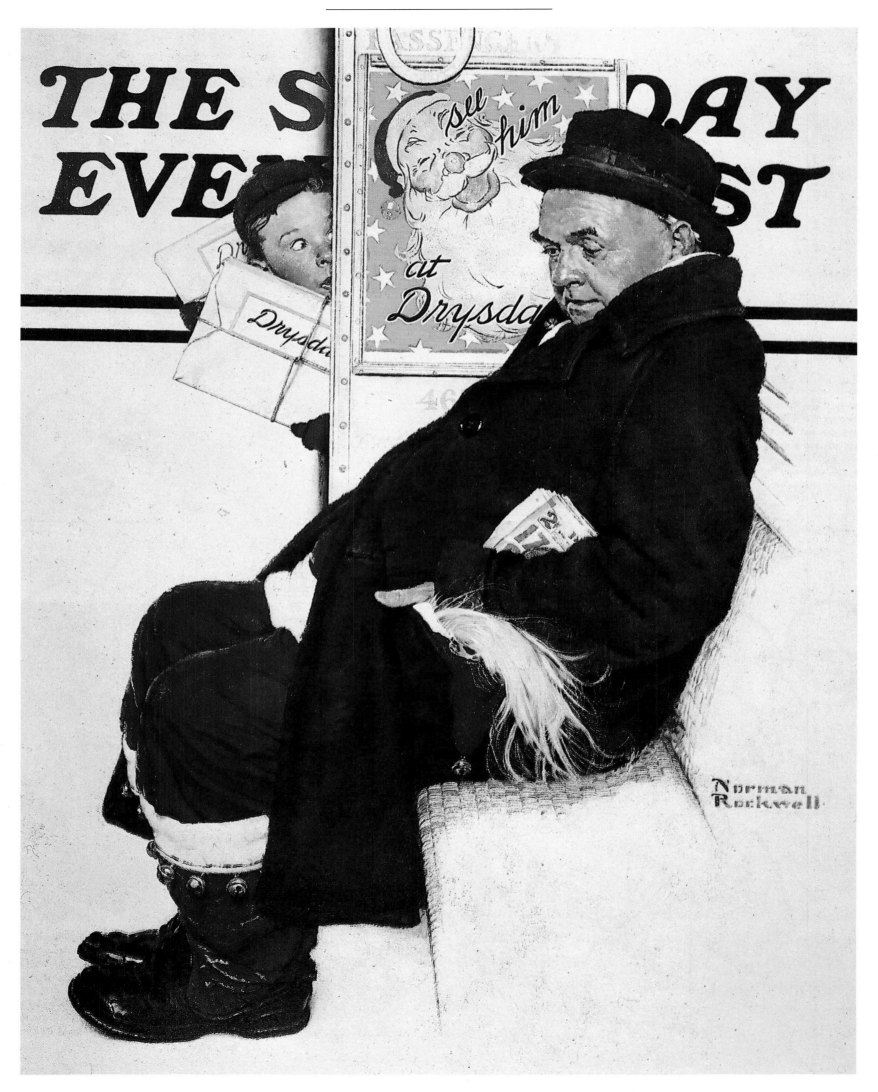

Santa on a Subway Train
Original oil painting for a *Post* cover, 28 December 1940

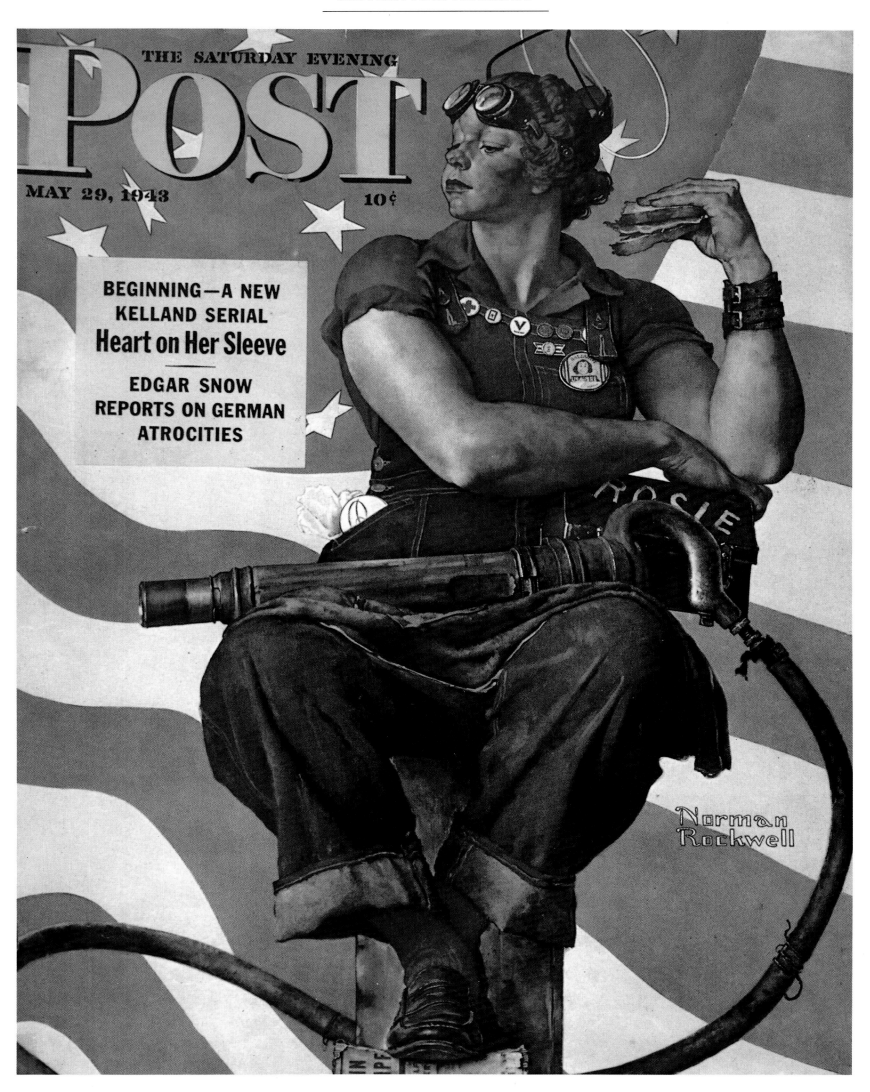

Rosie the Riveter
Post cover, 29 May 1943

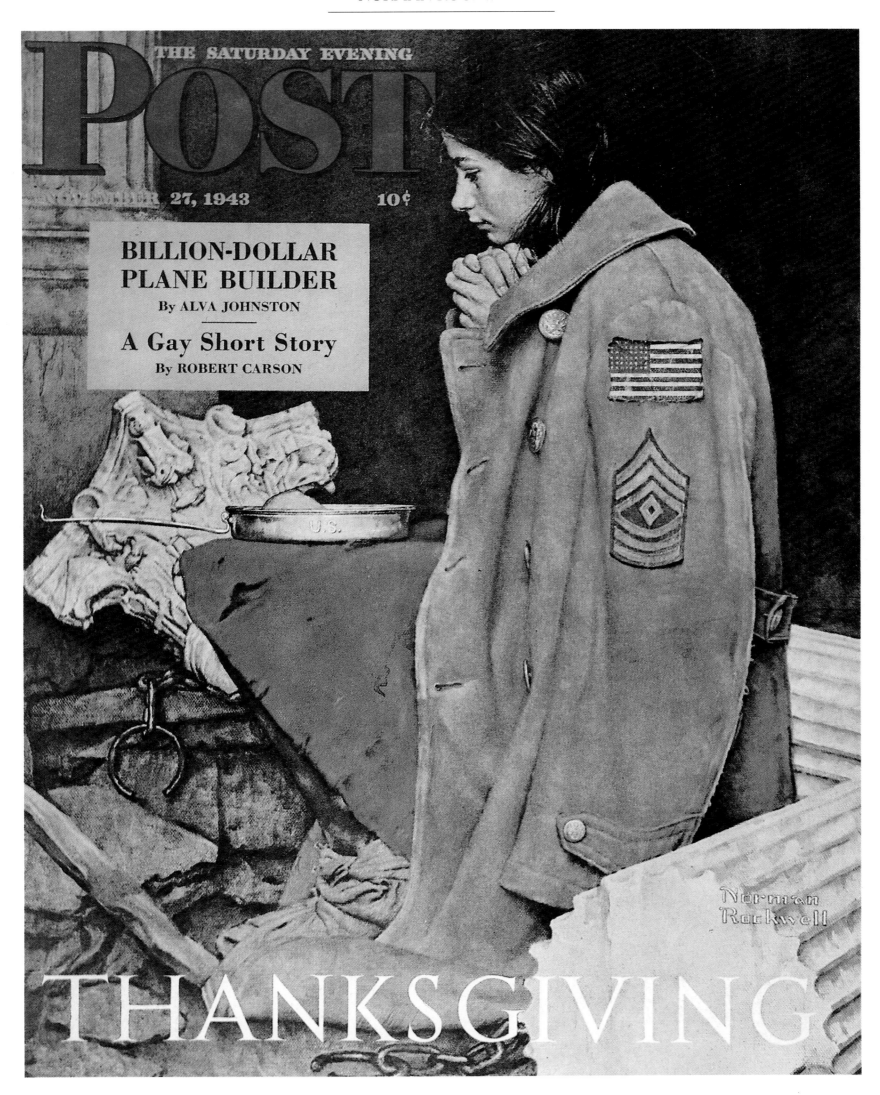

THE SATURDAY EVENING
POST
NOVEMBER 27, 1943   10¢

BILLION-DOLLAR
PLANE BUILDER
By ALVA JOHNSTON

A Gay Short Story
By ROBERT CARSON

THANKSGIVING

Norman Rockwell

Thanksgiving
Post cover, 27 November 1943

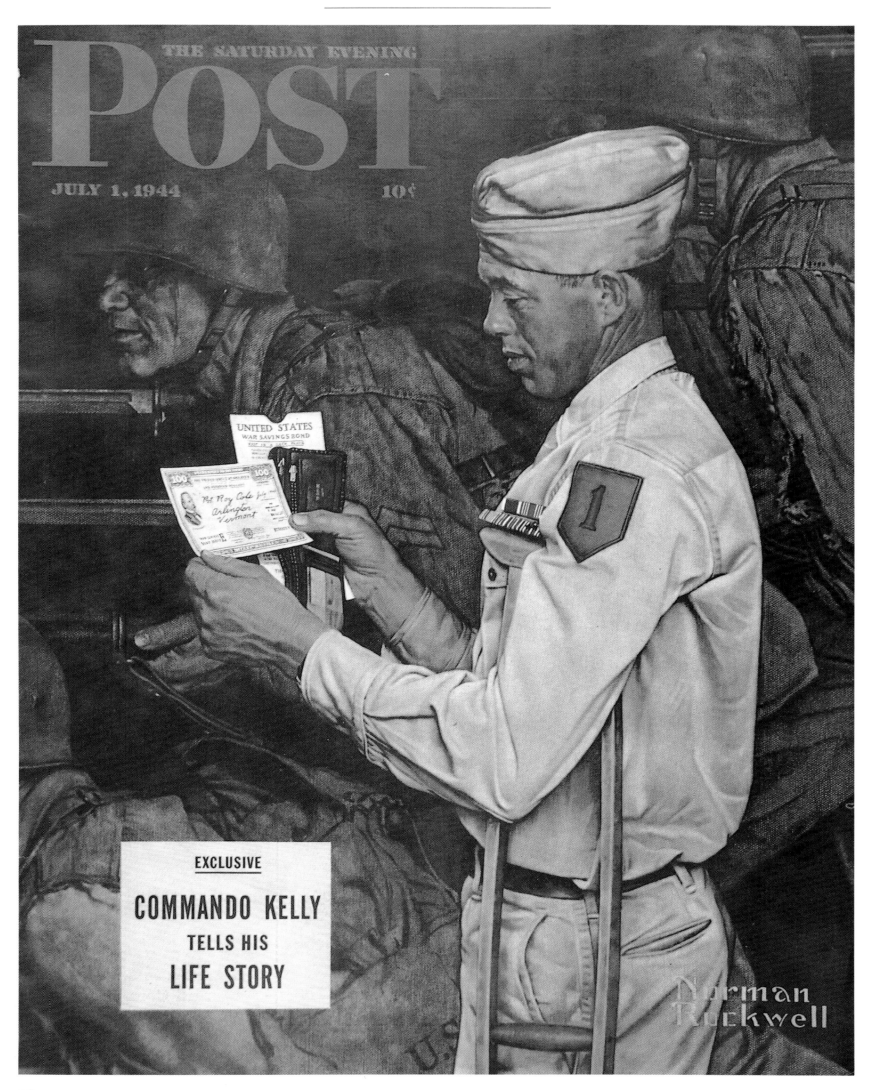

The War Savings Bond
Post cover, 1 July 1944

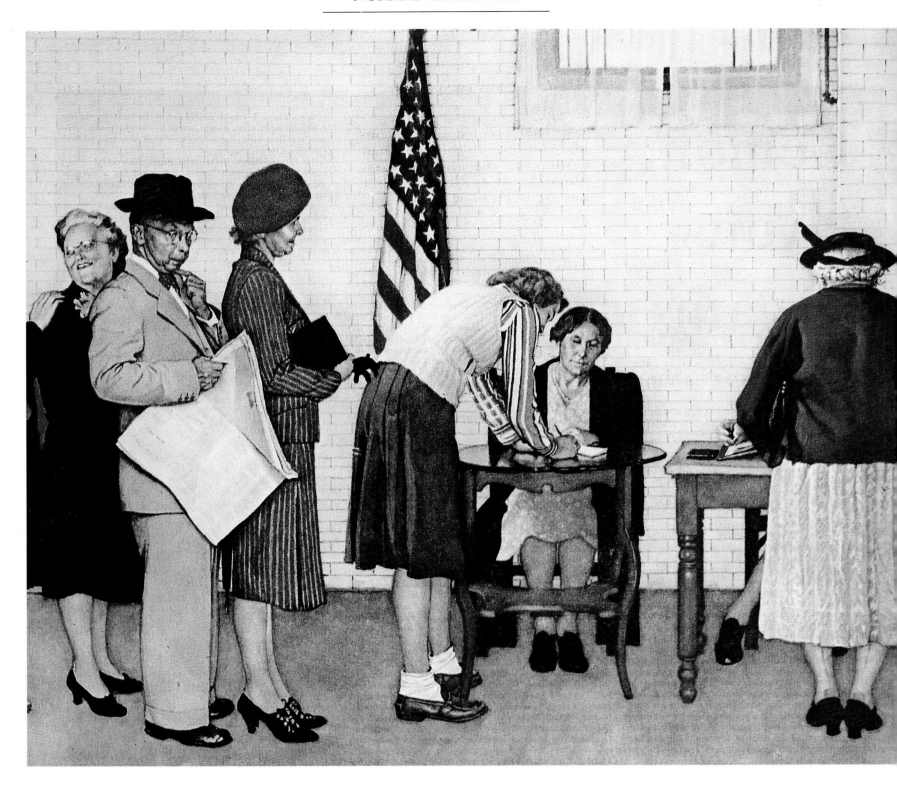

Norman Rockwell Paints America at the Polls
Post illustration, 4 November 1944

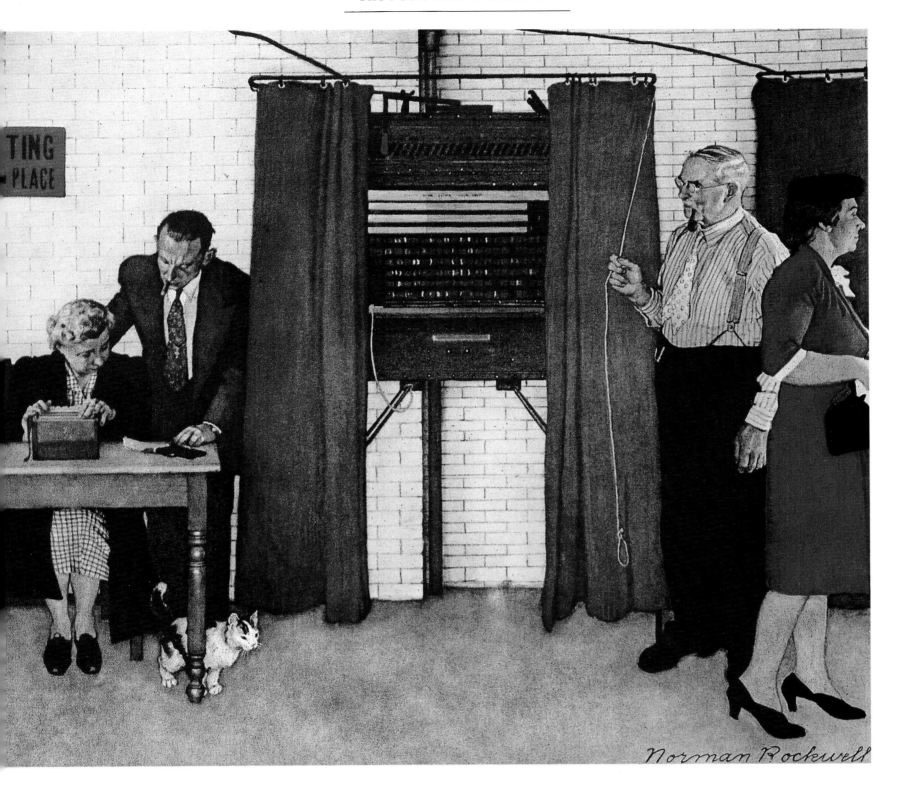

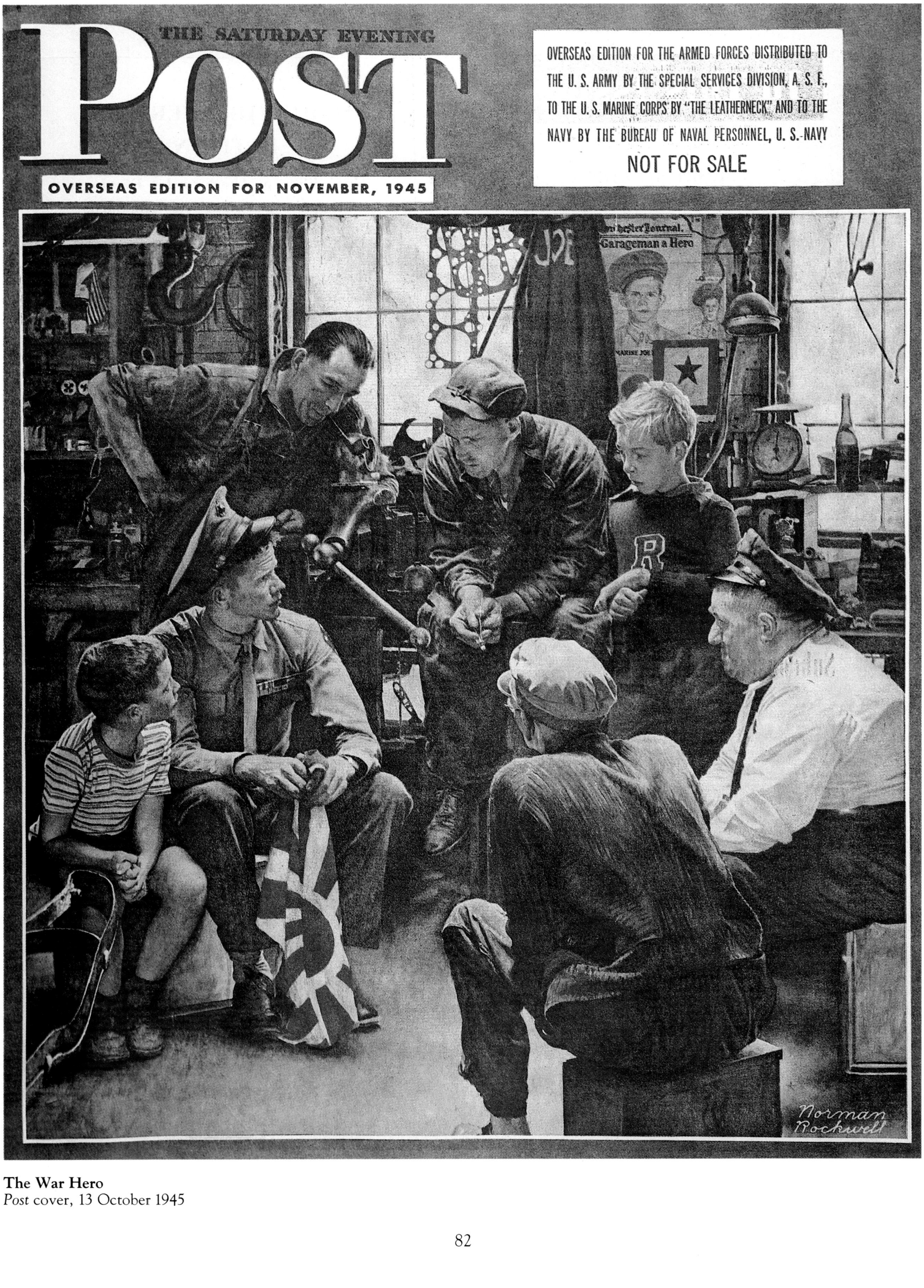

The War Hero
Post cover, 13 October 1945

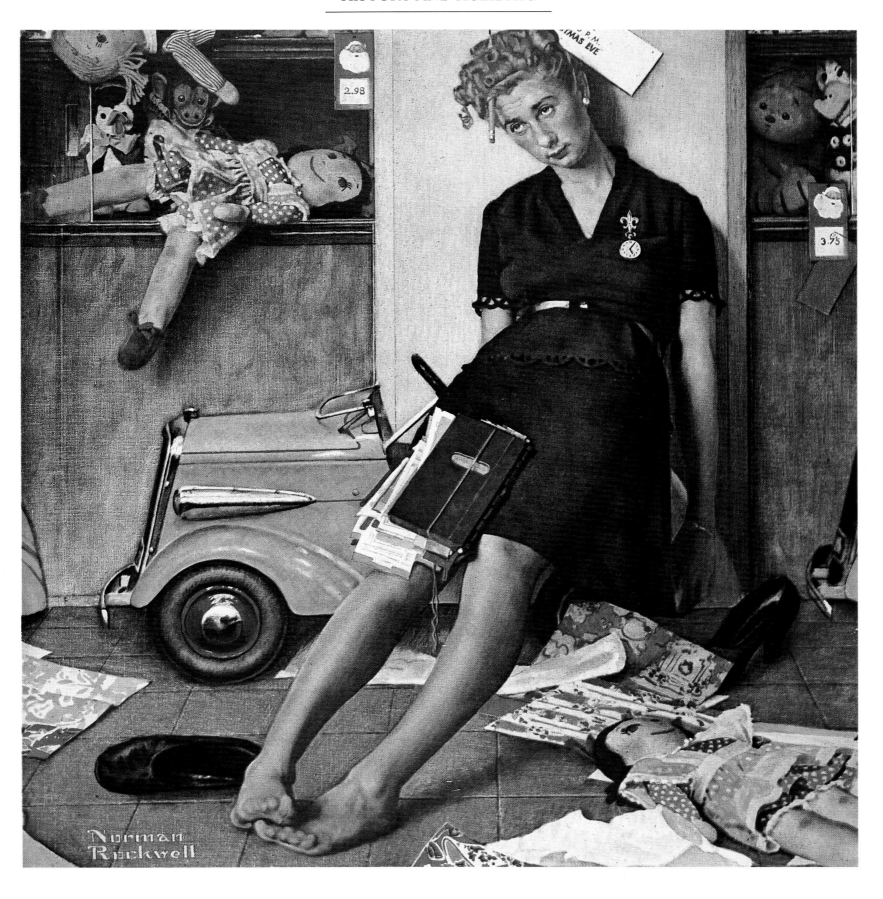

After the Christmas Rush
Post cover, 27 December 1947

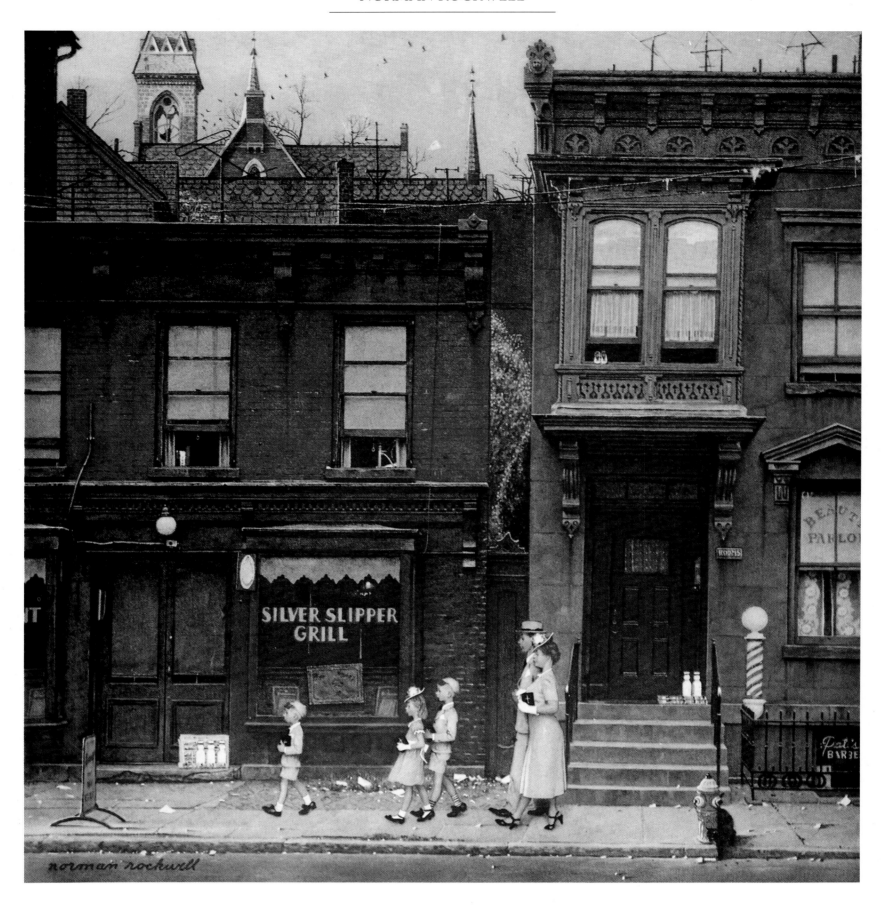

Walking to Church
Post cover, 4 April 1953

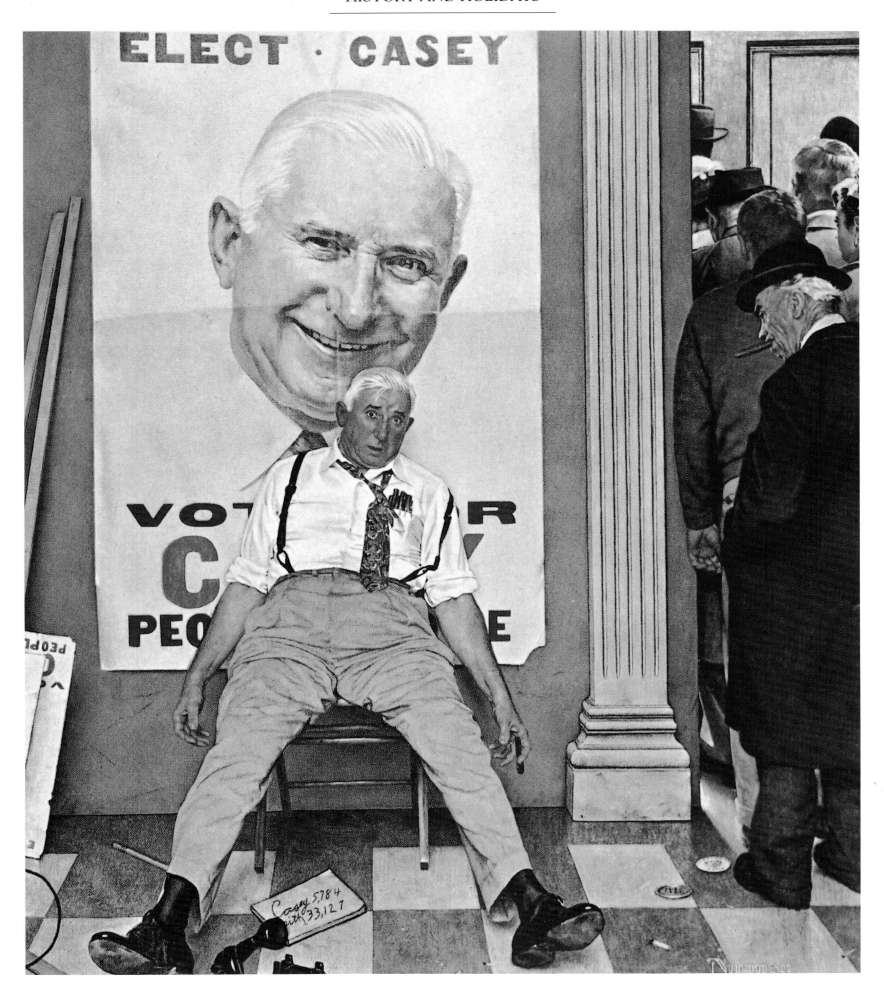

Elect Casey
Post cover, 8 November 1958

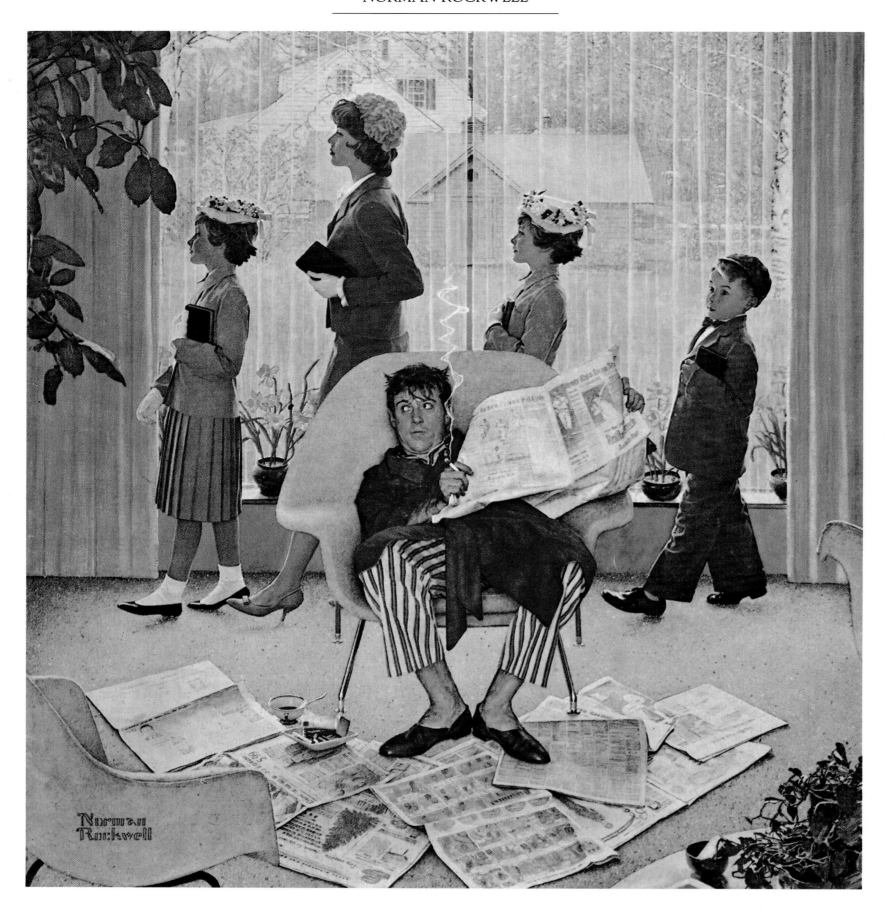

Easter Morning
Post cover, 16 May 1959

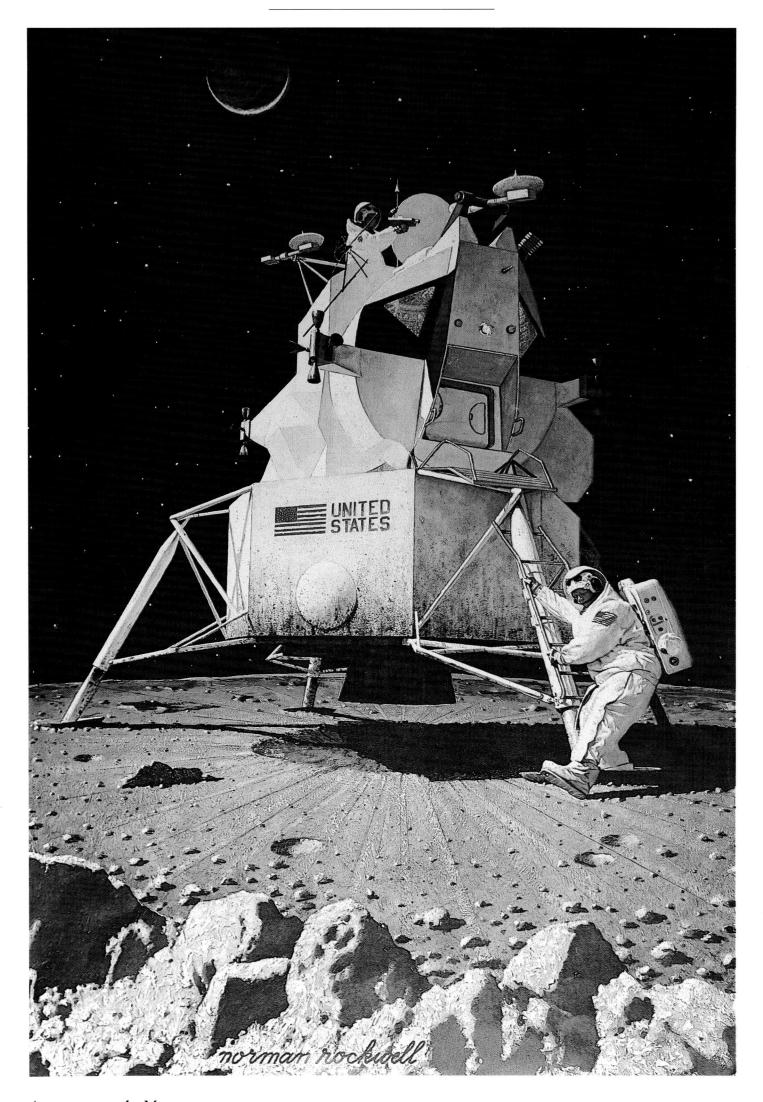

Astronauts on the Moon
Original oil painting for a *Look* illustration, 10 January 1967

PORTRAITS AND SOCIAL ISSUES

During World War II, Rockwell did some of his finest work, creating the figure of a representative G.I. to show the war through the eyes of one young soldier, his family, and the girl he'd left behind. Since Rockwell worked only from real models, or photographs of actual models, he needed to find someone to pose as his G.I., who would *not* likely be away at war. At a square dance in Arlington, Vermont, he found just the man: young Bob Buck, who had a draft deferment. Rockwell's wife Mary had just been reading *Wee Willie Winkie* to their children, and she came up with the idea of naming the G.I., Willie Gillis.

As soon as Willie Gillis began to appear on *Post* covers in 1941, Rockwell began to get letters from real Gillises, including a handful of Willies. Rockwell showed Willie getting a food package from home, being fussed over by two pretty girls at the USO, and Willie on K.P. duty and on leave. Then, in 1943, Bob Buck decided to forego his draft exemption and enlist in the navy. Before Buck left for the Pacific, Rockwell took photos of Buck from every imaginable angle and was able to keep the series going through the war and thereafter. When Buck returned to Arlington after the war, Rockwell painted his last Willie Gillis cover: *Willie Gillis in College*. Rockwell showed Willie's helmet and service discharge in his dorm room and gave him a view of the Williams College belltower from his window. For years after the war, Rockwell continued to get letters from Gillises asking how Willie was doing.

It was also during the war that Rockwell completed what became his most famous set of paintings, *The Four Freedoms*, depicting *Freedom of Speech, Freedom of Worship, Freedom from Want*, and *Freedom from Fear*. Rockwell got his idea from Roosevelt and Churchill's Atlantic Charter, which stated that the war was being fought to preserve four basic freedoms. Both Rockwell and his Arlington friend and fellow artist, Mead Schaeffer, wanted to help in the war effort; the two took some sketches to the U.S. War Department in Washington – only to have their good intentions dismissed by an official who reminded them that "there's a war on," and implied that there was no place for artists in the front line of the war effort.

Schaeffer and Rockwell then went to the *Post*, where editor Ben Hibbs suggested that Schaeffer concentrate on a series of *Post* covers showing combat scenes. Rockwell was commissioned to do *The Four Freedoms*, the project which occupied him for the next seven months. The project was Rockwell's most ambitious; when it was done, he remarked that "it should have been tackled by Michelangelo." Still, Rockwell's *Four Freedoms* were reproduced more than any other paintings in the world and spearheaded an enormously successful U.S. war bond drive.

The Four Freedoms, along with such later Rockwell works as *The Golden Rule, The Peace Corps in Ethiopia*, and *The Problem We All Live With*, revealed Rockwell's abilities as a "serious" artist. Rockwell himself never deviated from his pride in being "merely" an illustrator. Yet, much of his work – including portraits like *Triple Self-Portrait*, and the paintings of most major twentieth-century American political leaders – revealed that Rockwell, the illustrator, was Rockwell the American artist.

Triple Self-Portrait
Post cover, 13 February 1960

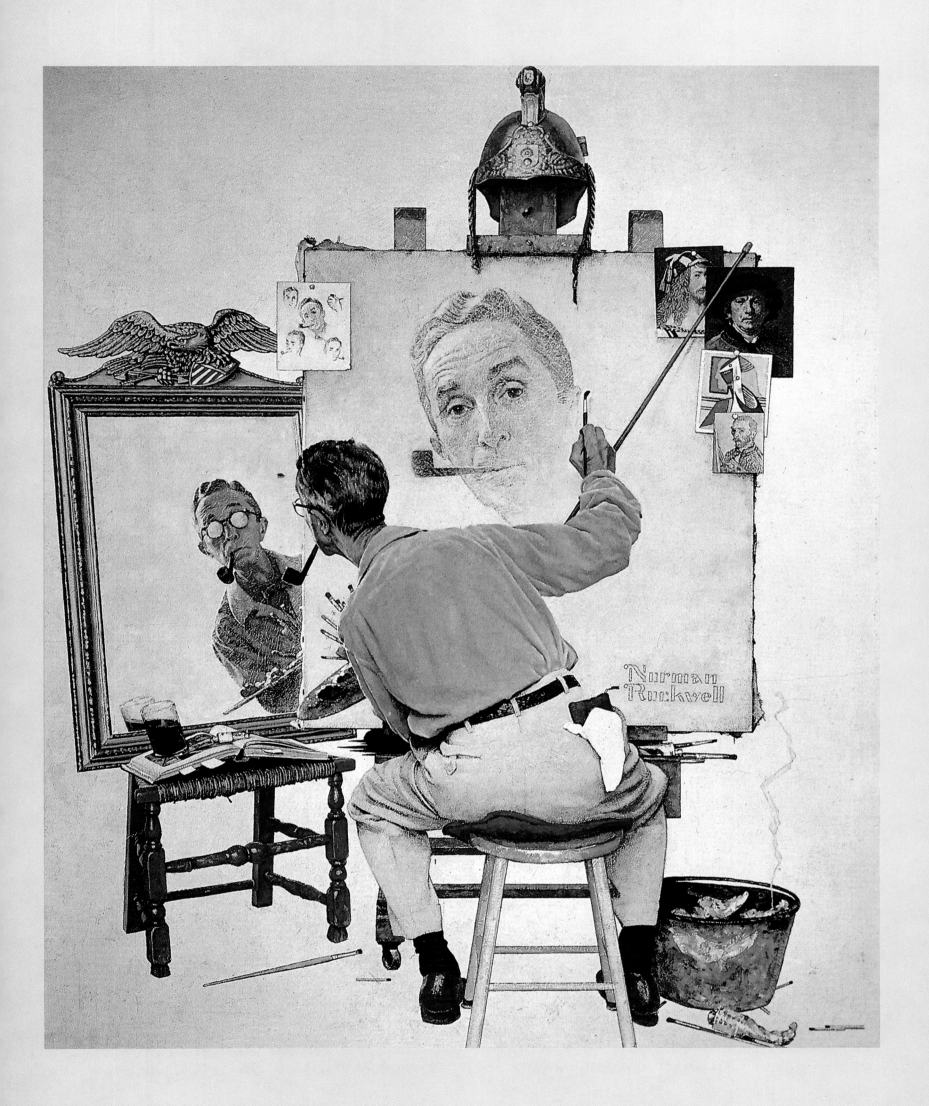

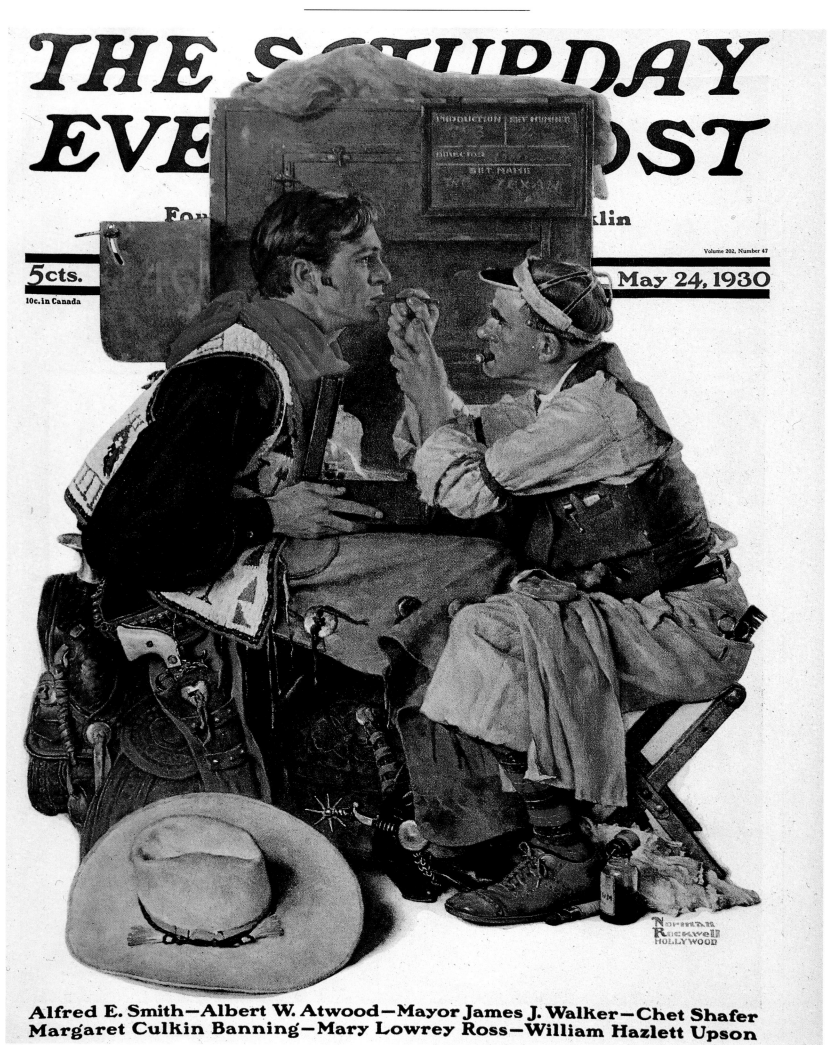

Gary Cooper
Post cover, 24 May 1930

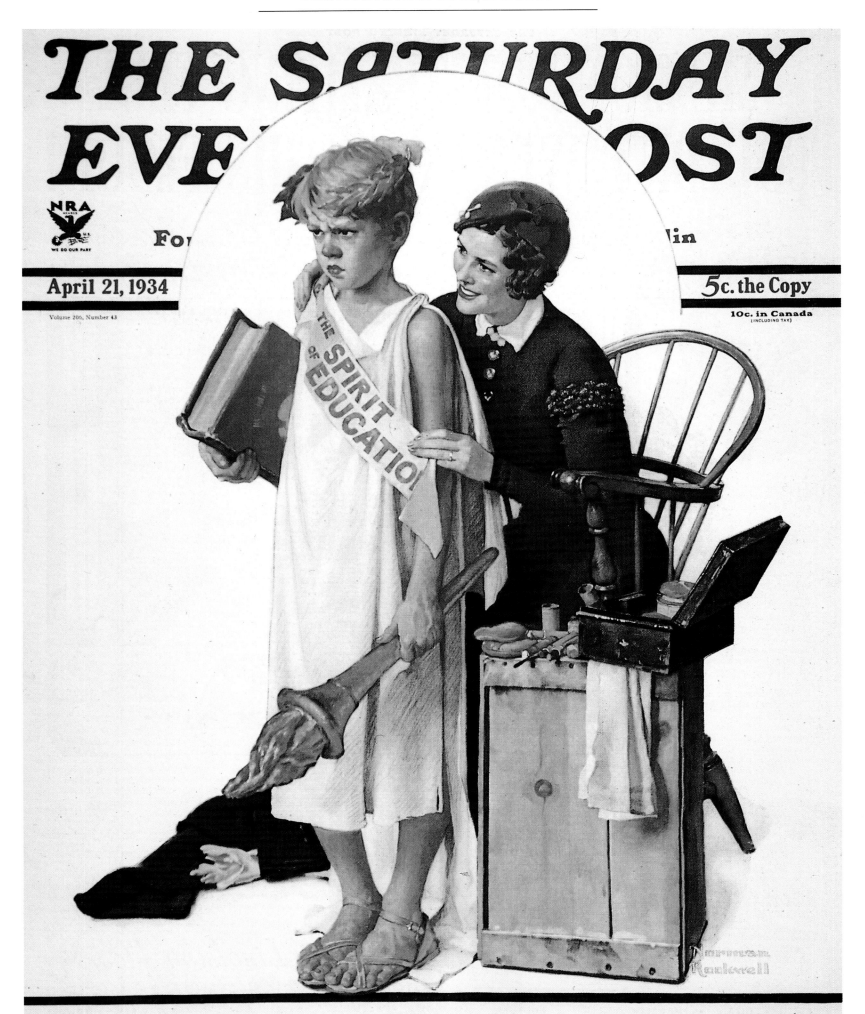

The Spirit of Education
Post cover, 21 April 1934

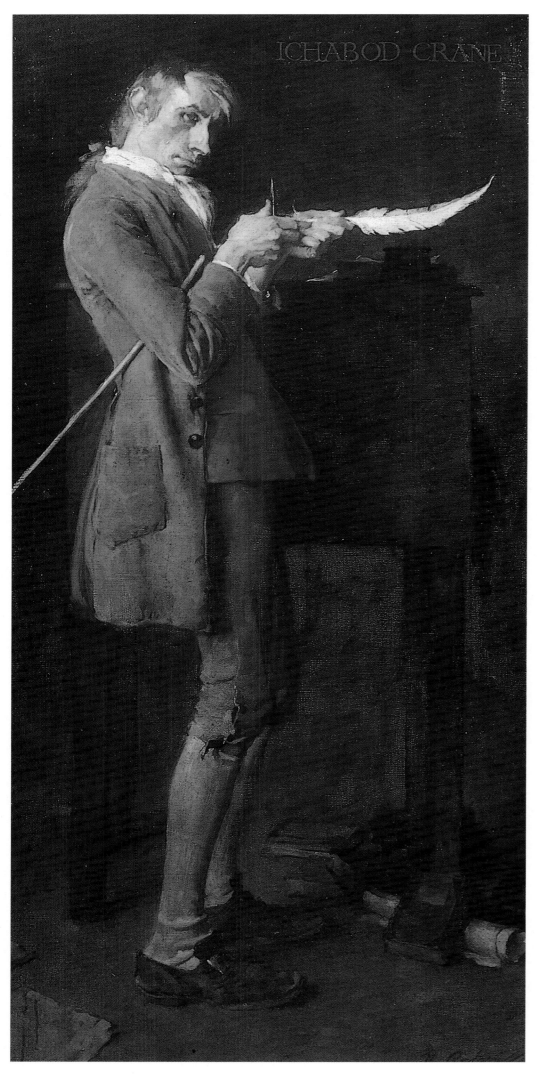

Ichabod Crane
Original oil painting (unused as illustration, undated)

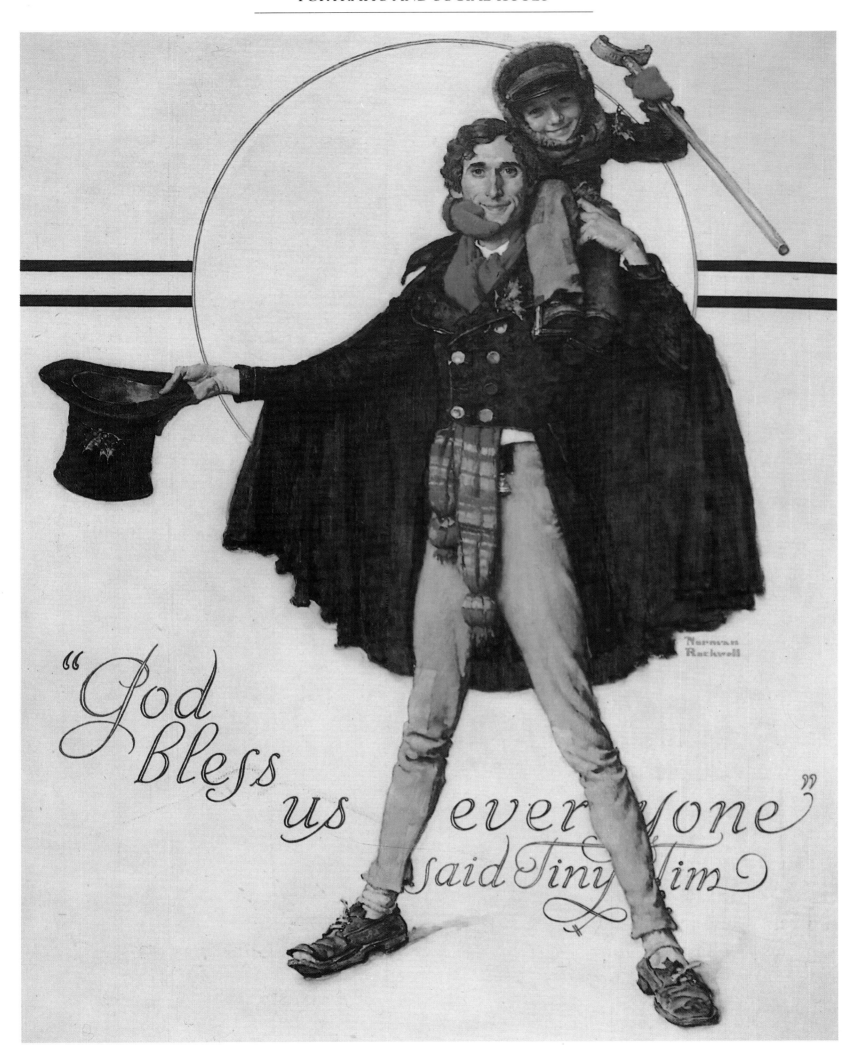

Tiny Tim and Bob Cratchit
Original oil painting for a *Post* cover, 15 December 1934

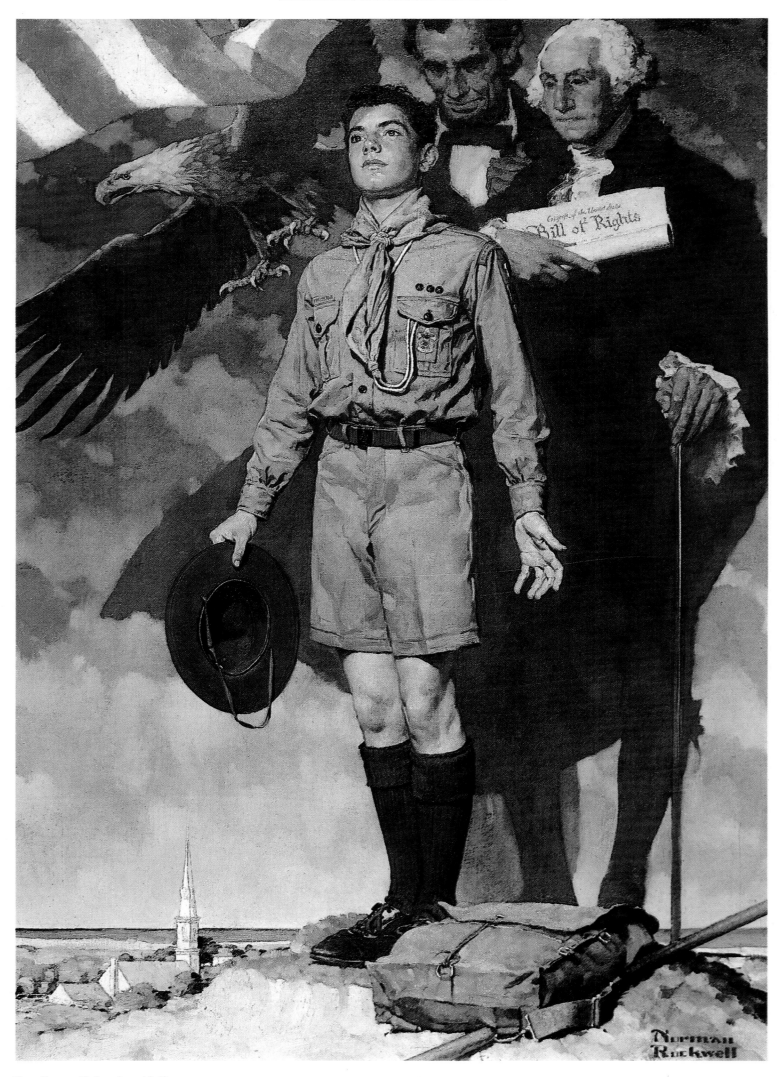

Boy Scout Calendar, 1942
Produced from art archives, Brown & Bigelow
Permission Boy Scouts of America

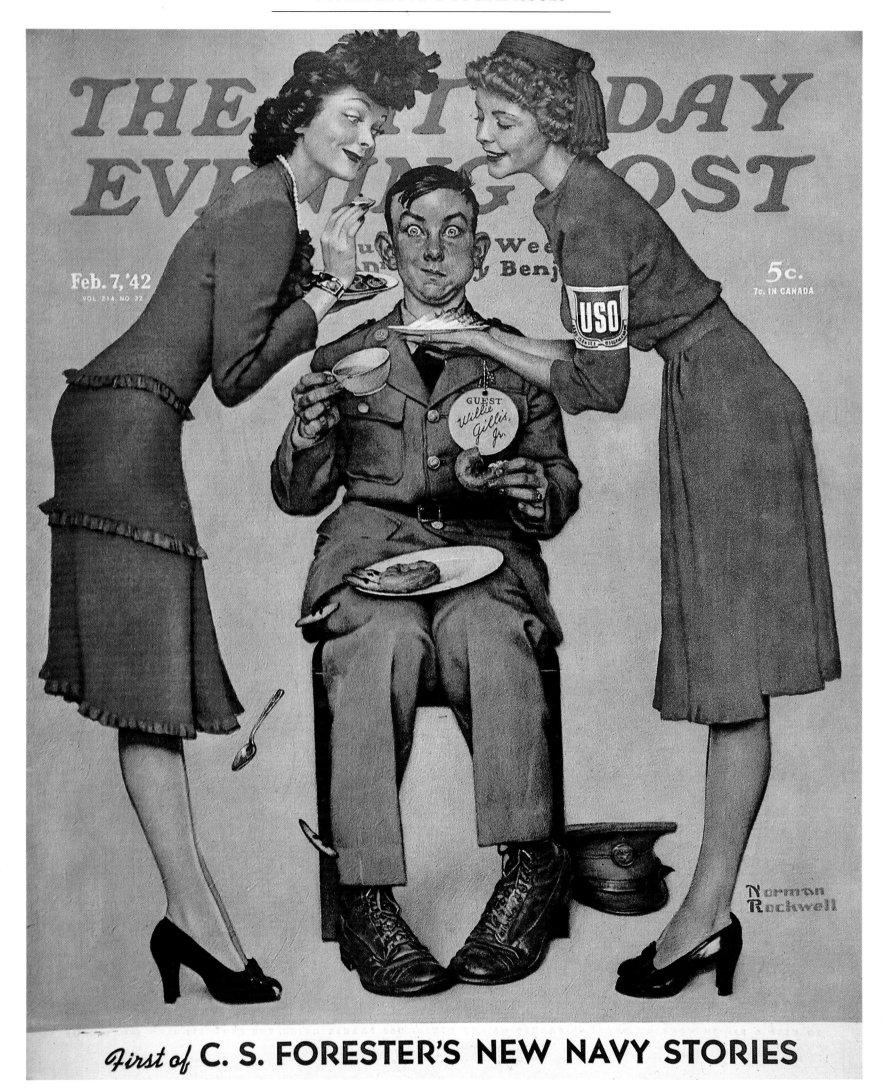

Willie Gillis at the USO
Post cover, 7 February 1942

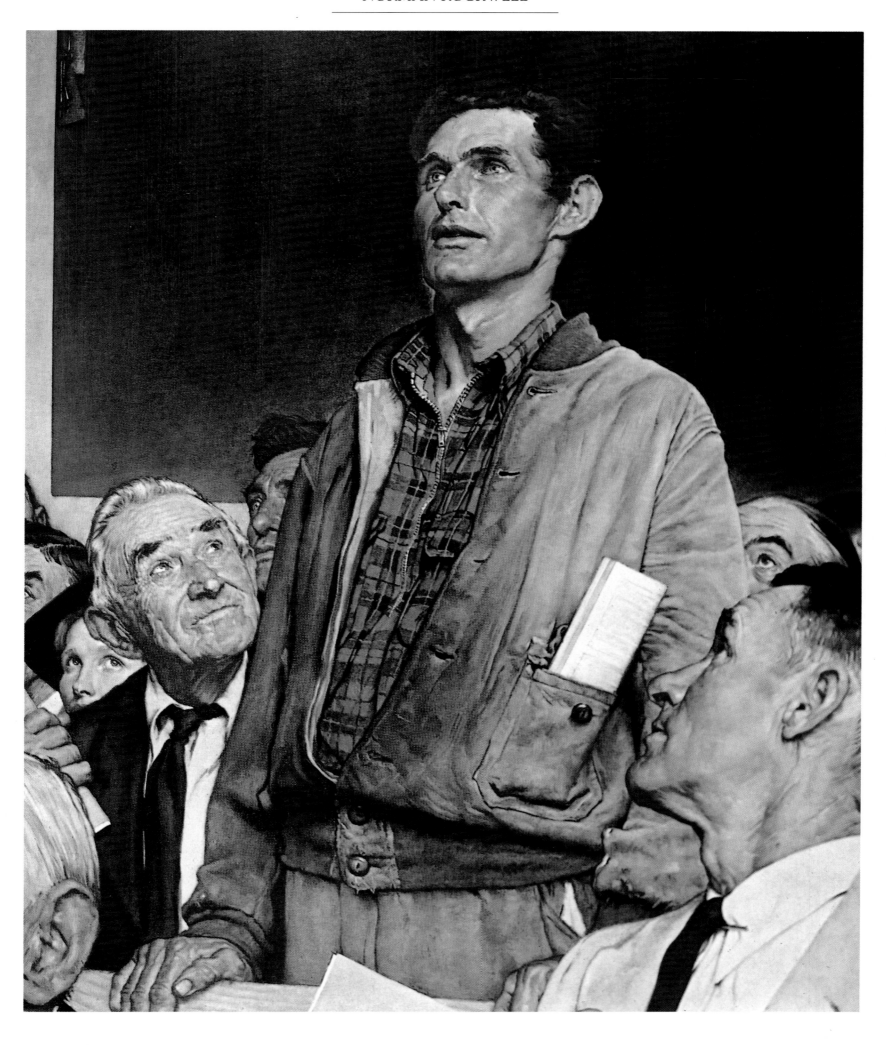

The Four Freedoms: Freedom of Speech
Original oil painting for a poster, 1943

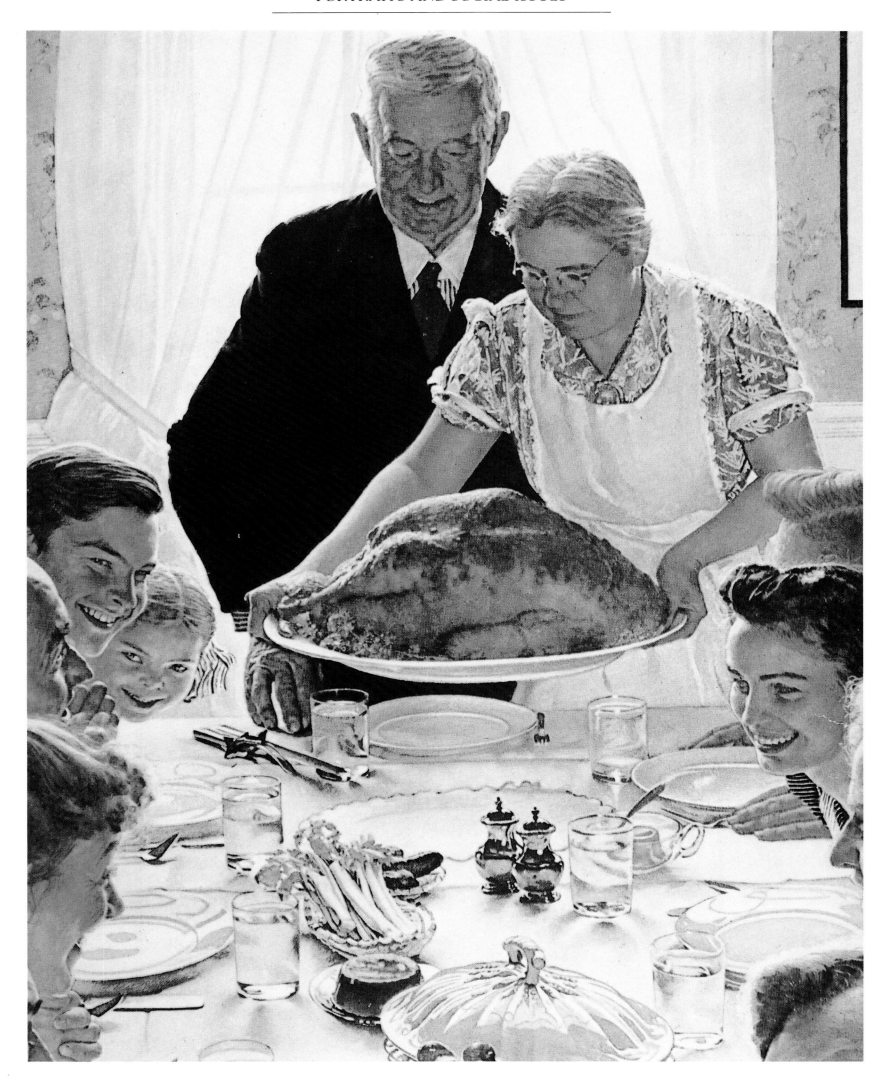

The Four Freedoms: Freedom from Want
Original oil painting for a poster, 1943

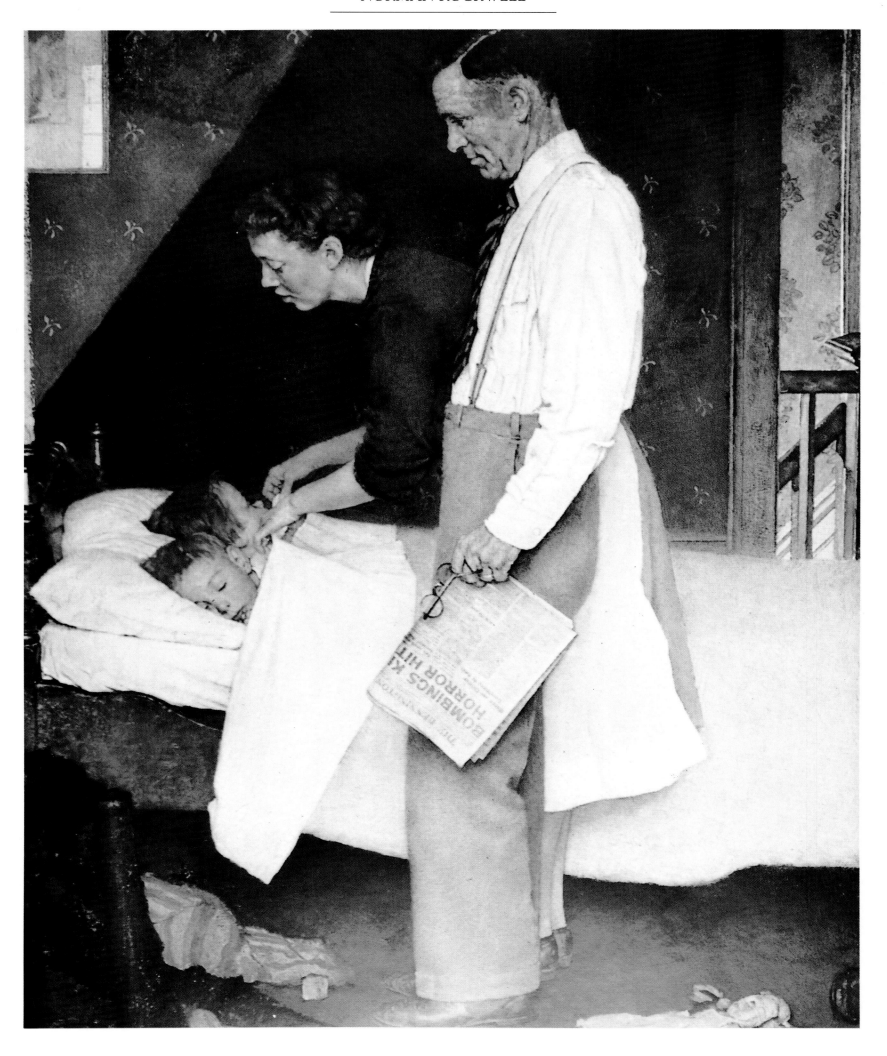

The Four Freedoms: Freedom from Fear
Original oil painting for a poster, 1943

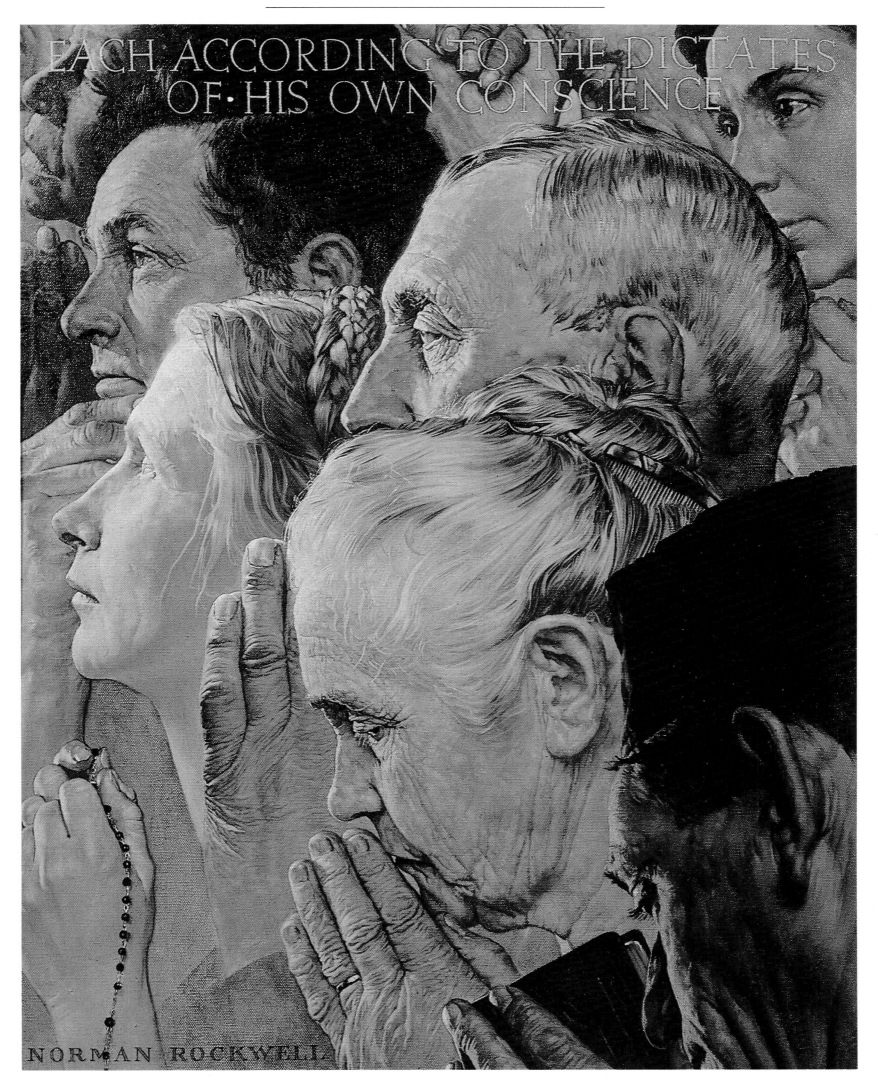

The Four Freedoms: Freedom of Worship
Original oil painting for a poster, 1943

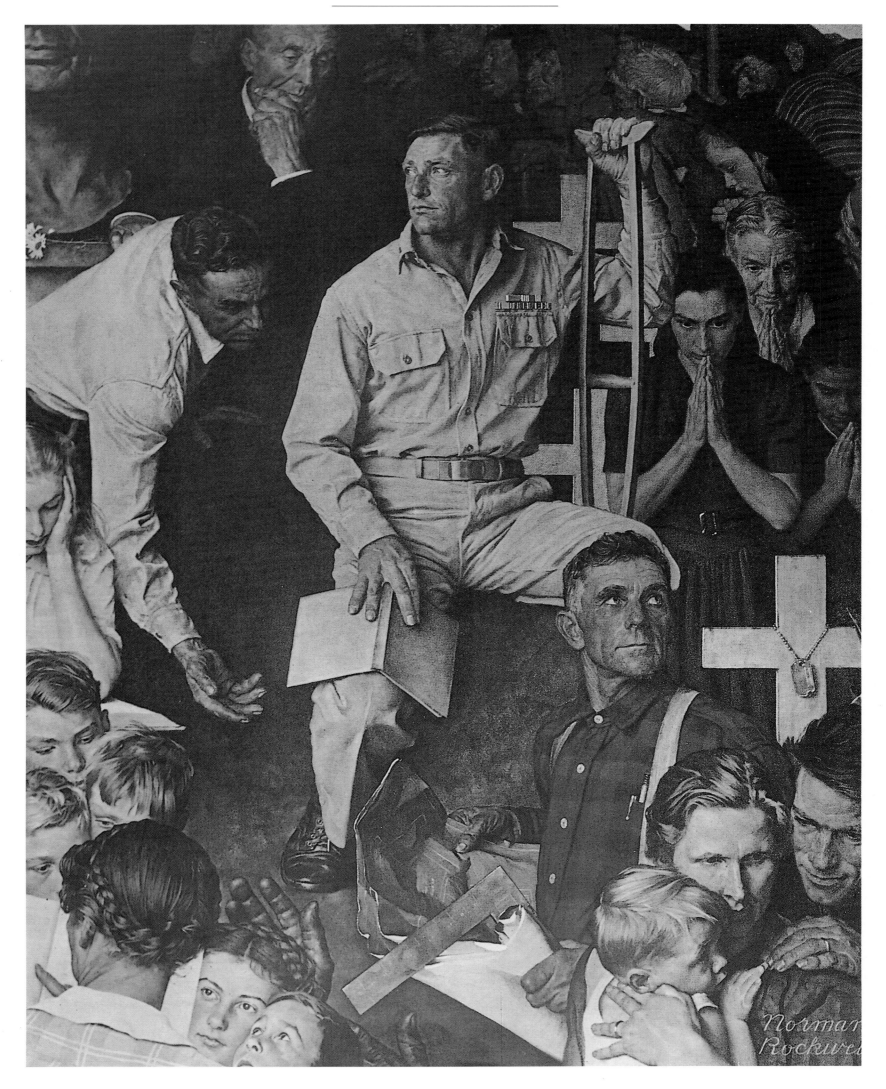

The Long Shadow of Lincoln
Post illustration for a poem, 10 February 1945

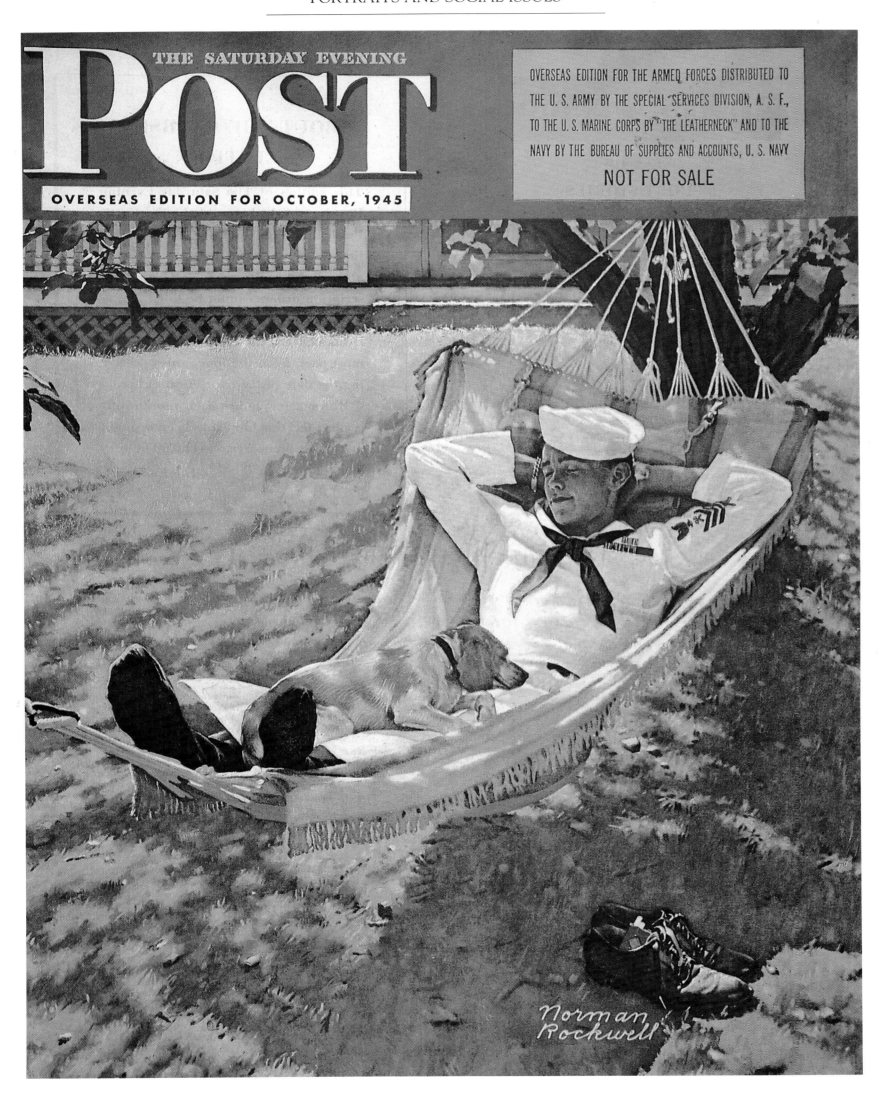

Willie Gillis on Leave
Post cover, 15 September 1945

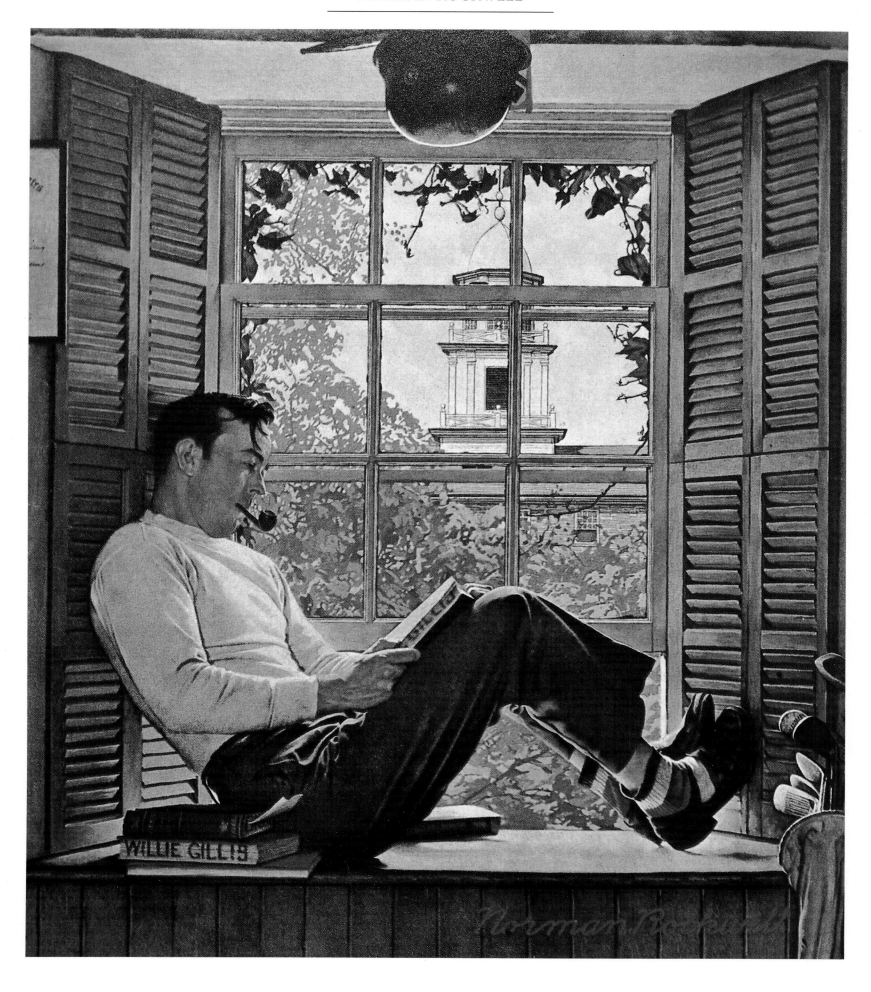

Willie Gillis in College
Original oil painting for a *Post* cover, 5 October 1946

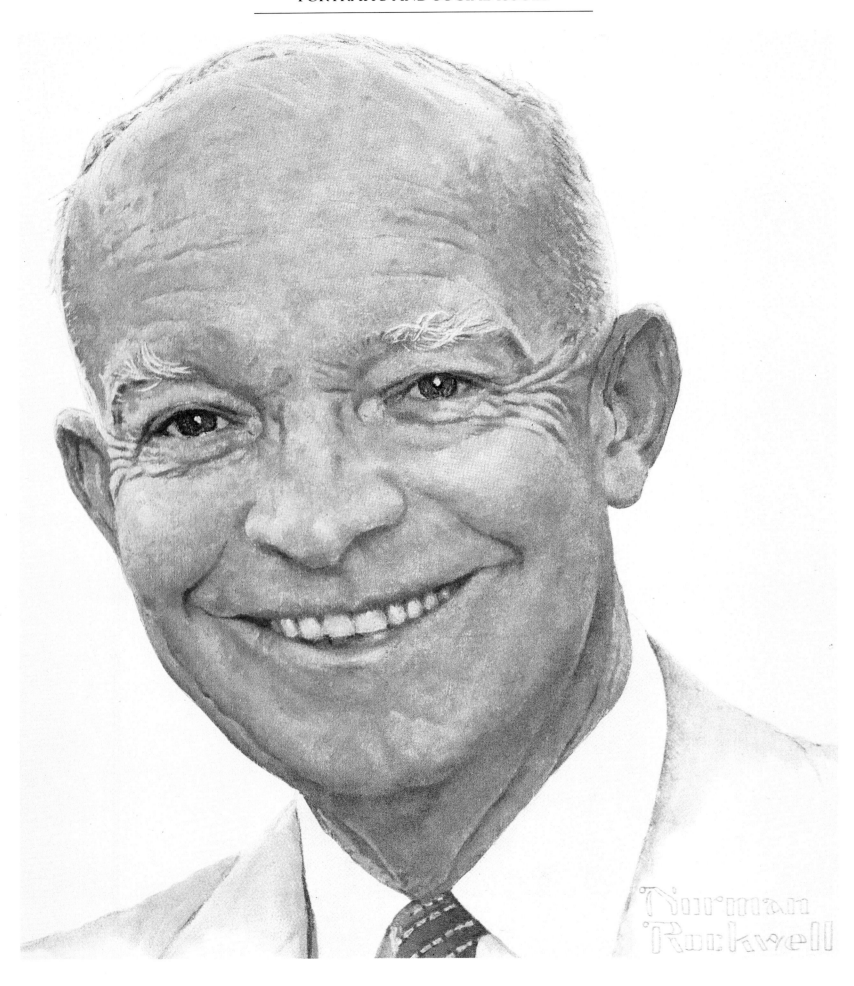

Dwight D. Eisenhower
Post cover, 13 October 1956

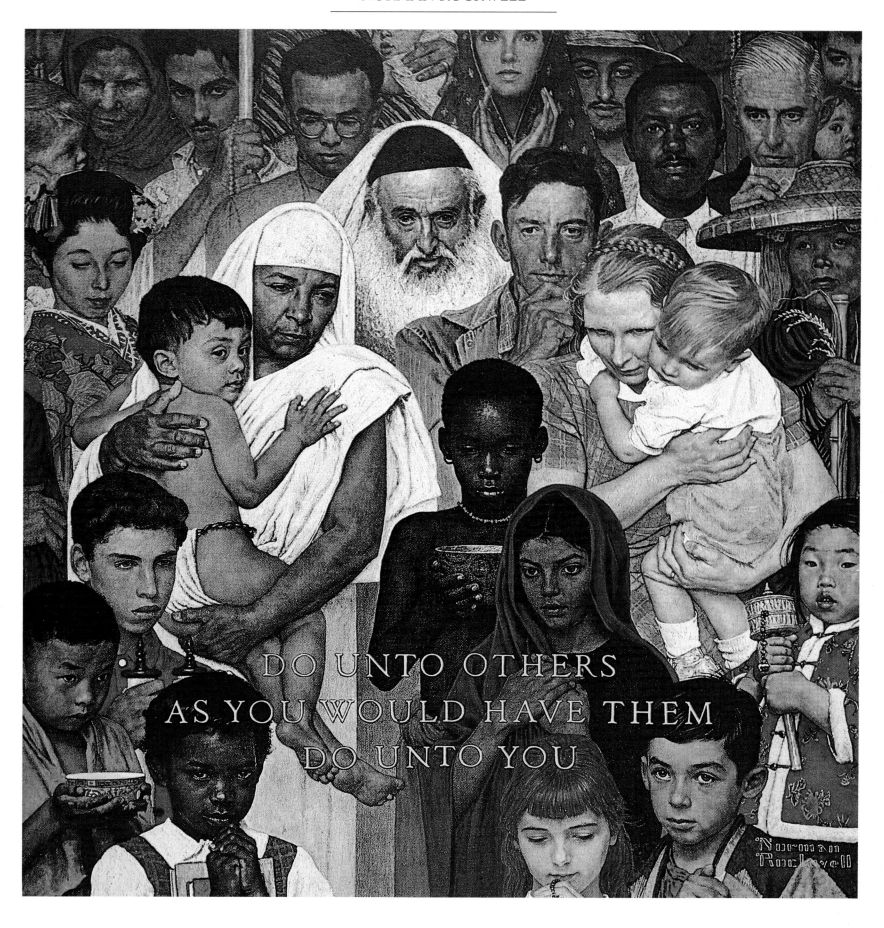

The Golden Rule
Post cover, 1 April 1961

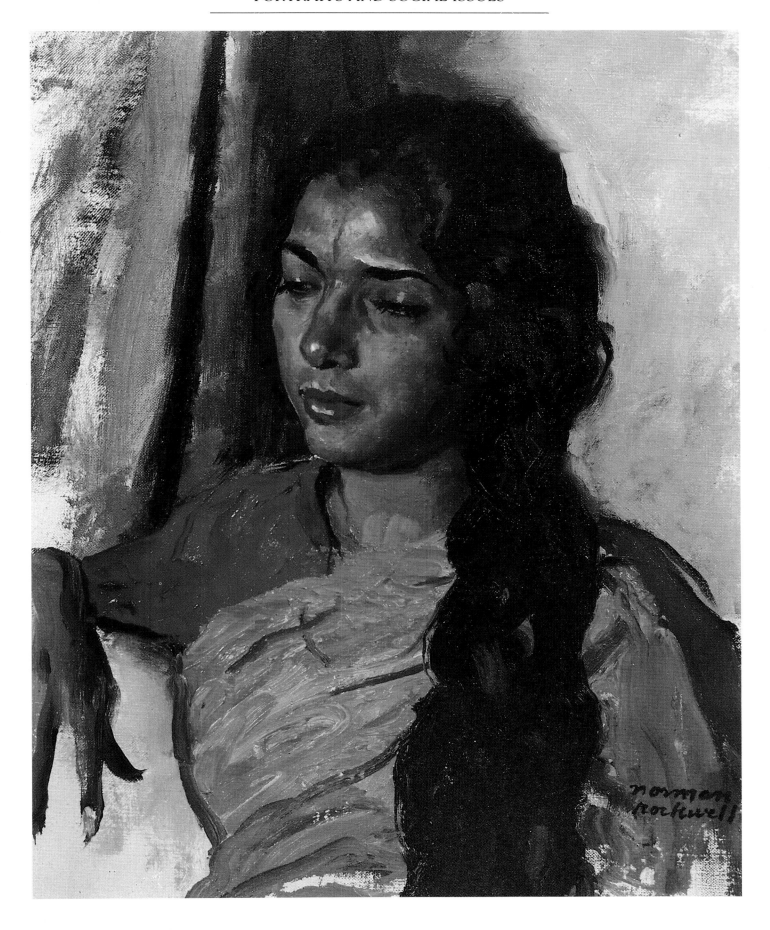

An Indian Art Student
American Artist illustration, September 1964
(Original portrait painted 1962.)

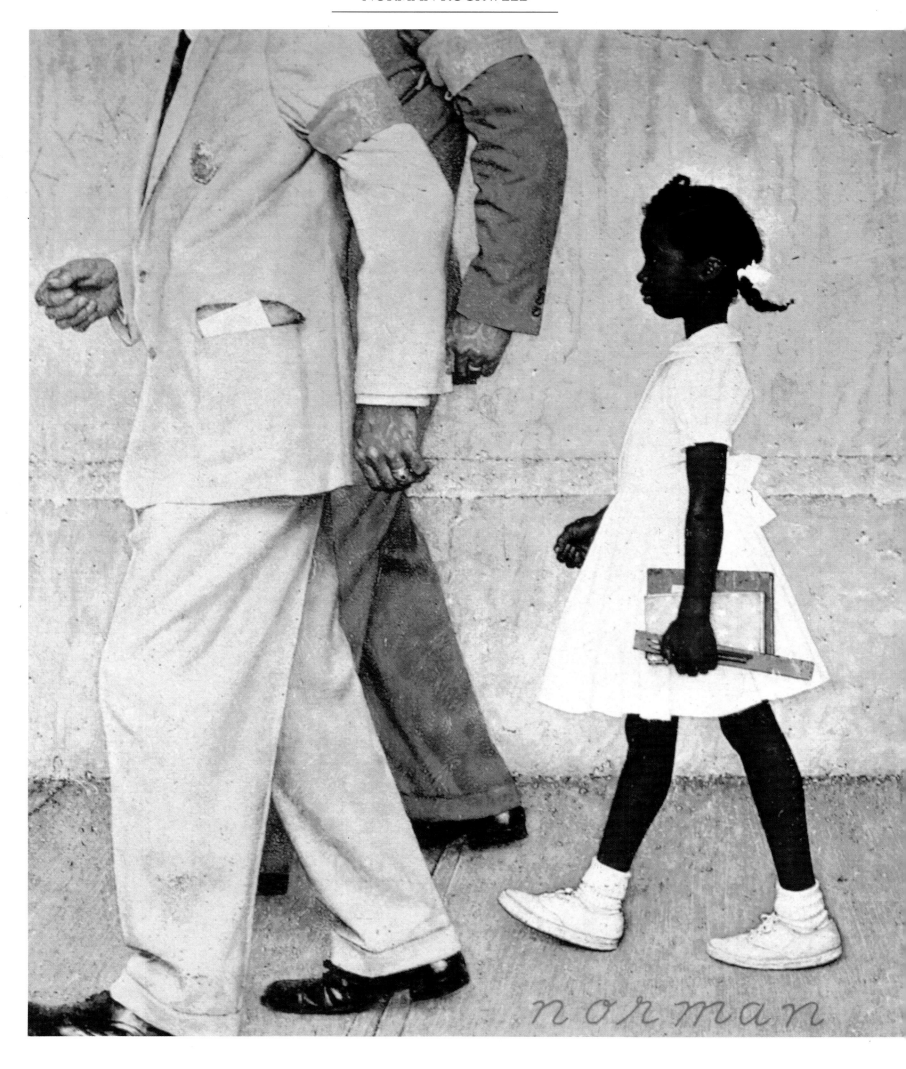

The Problem We All Live With
Look illustration, 14 January 1964

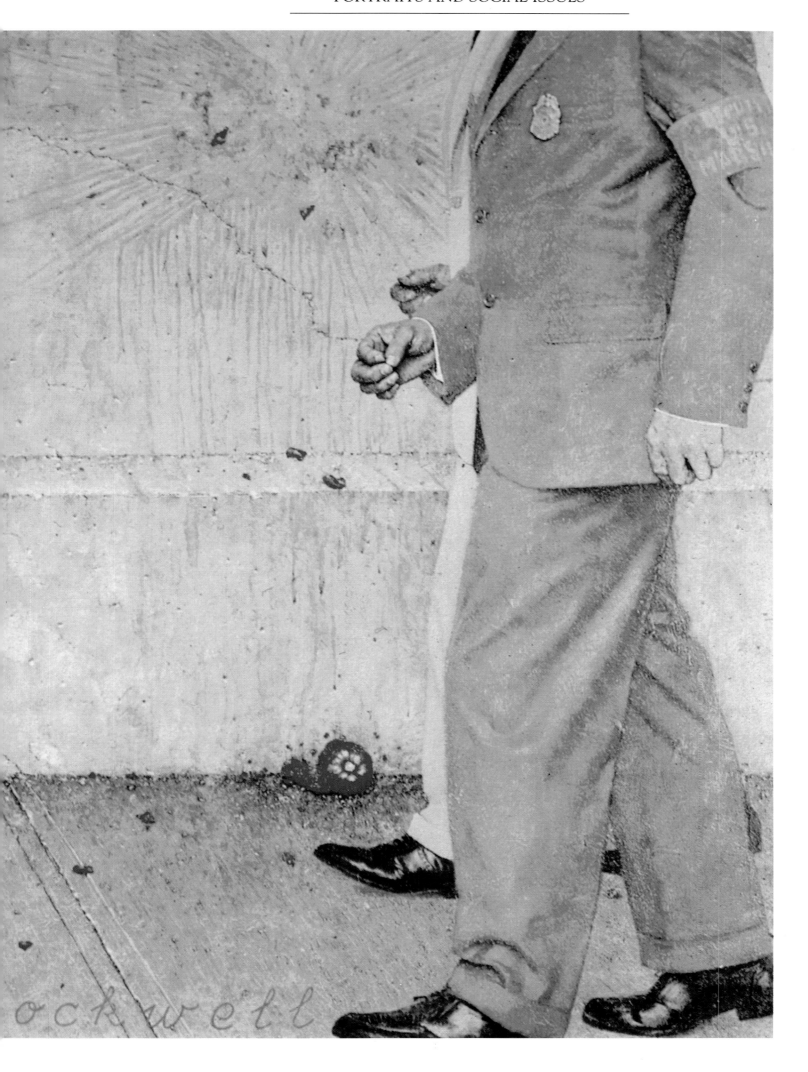

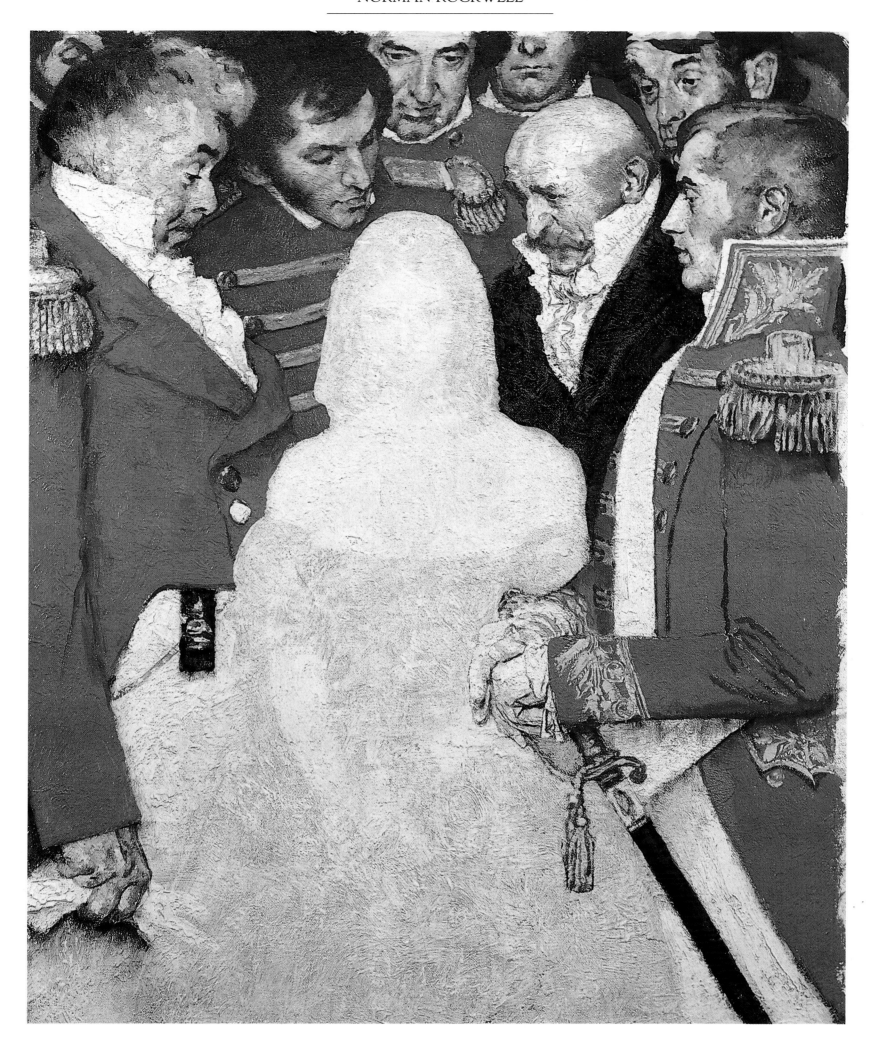

Becky Sharp
Original oil painting (unused as illustration), 1965.
(White overpainting by the artist.)

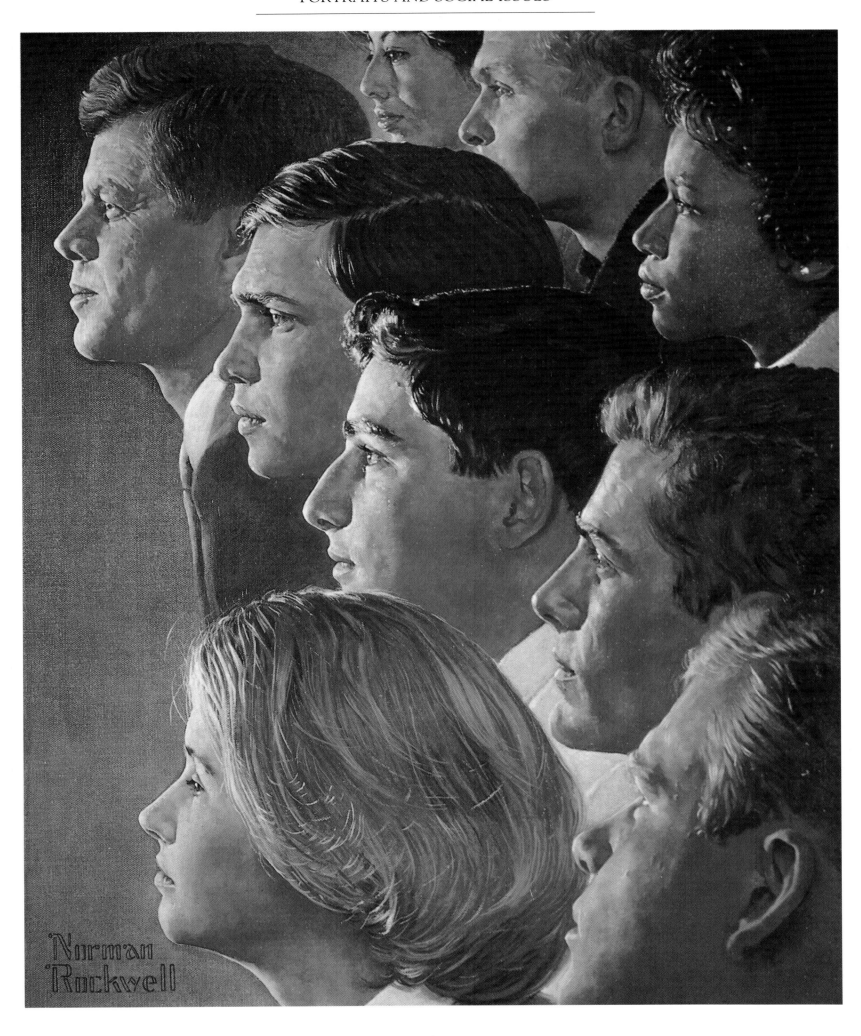

John Kennedy and the Peace Corps
Original oil painting for a *Look* cover, 14 June 1966

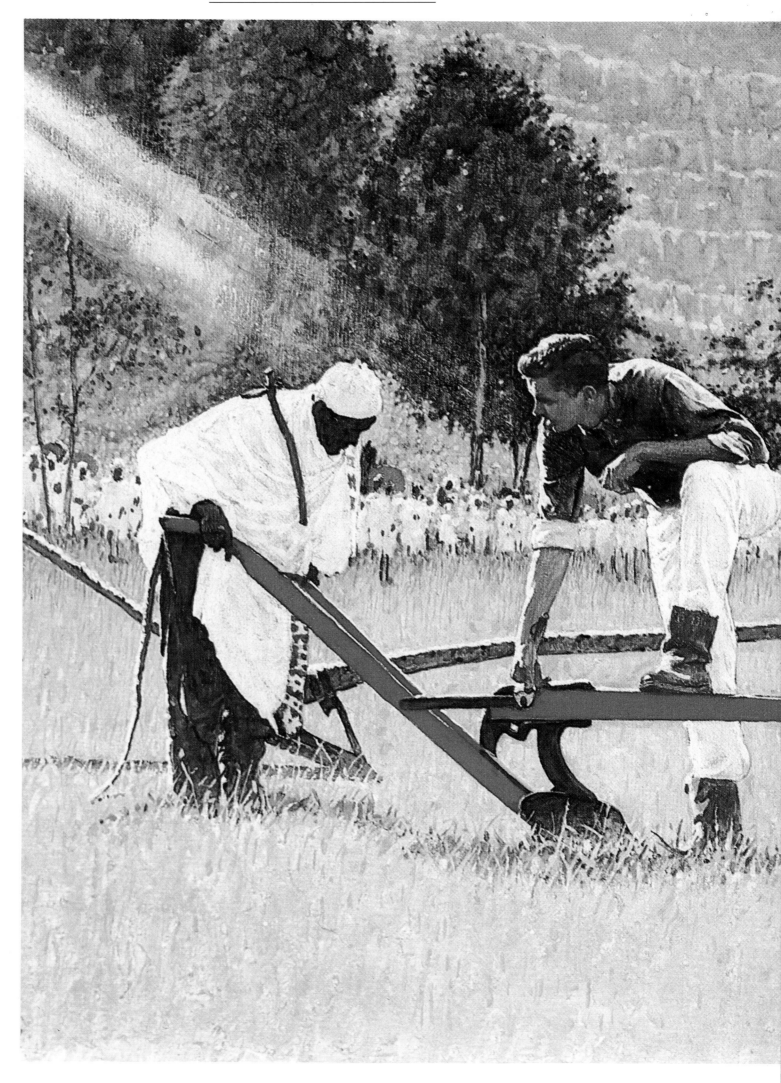

The Peace Corps in Ethiopia
Look illustration, 14 June 1966

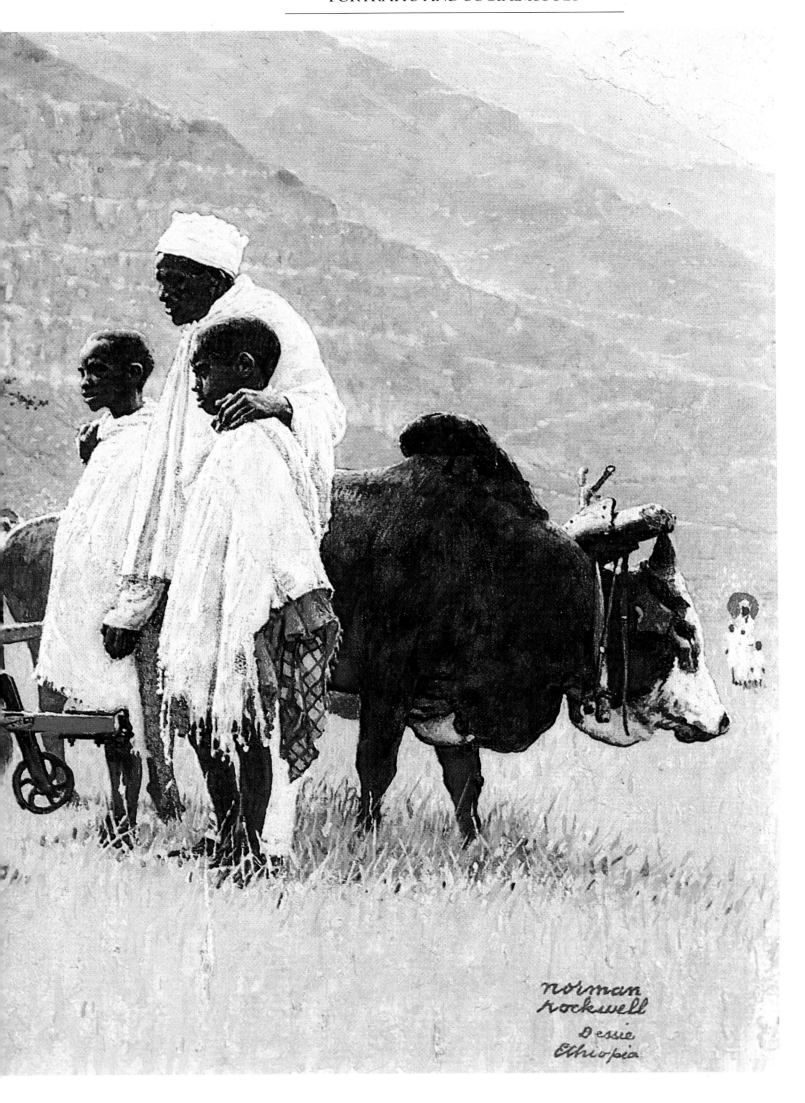

LIST OF COLOR PLATES

After the Christmas Rush	83
After the Prom	39
Airplane Trip	33
Artist and Critic	18
Artist Faced with Blank Canvas	11
Astronauts on the Moon	87
Becky Sharp	108
Ben Franklin Signing the Declaration of Independence	73
The Bodybuilder	24
Boy with Carriage	10
Boy Scout Calendar, 1942	94
Breaking Home Ties	63
Christmas . . . Sing Merrilie	72
Commuters	55
The Connoisseur	19
Couple in Rumbleseat	31
Cousin Reginald Plays Pirate	22
Day in the Life of a Little Boy	36
Day in the Life of a Little Girl	37
The Diving Board	58
Doctor and Doll	28
Dreams of Chivalry	27
The Dugout	60
Dwight D. Eisenhower	103
Easter Morning	86
Elect Casey	85
A Family Tree	4
Fixing a Flat	54
The Four Freedoms: Freedom from Fear	98
The Four Freedoms: Freedom of Speech	96
The Four Freedoms: Freedom from Want	97
The Four Freedoms: Freedom of Worship	99
Gary Cooper	90
Girl at the Mirror	21
The Golden Rule	104
The Gossips	35
Home for Thanksgiving	69
Ice Cream Carrier	34
Ichabod Crane	92
An Indian Art Student	105
Is He Coming?	70
John Kennedy and the Peace Corps	109
The Jury	65
The Long Shadow of Lincoln	100
Man Threading Needle	23
The Marriage License	64
Mary Barstow Rockwell	14
Maternity Waiting Room	50-51
Merrie Christmas	74
New Kids in the Neighborhood	66-67
No Swimming	43
Norman Rockwell Paints America at the Polls	80-81
Norman Rockwell Visits a Country Doctor	56-57
Norman Rockwell Visits a Country Editor	48-49
Norman Rockwell Visits a Country School	52-53
Norman Rockwell Visits a Ration Board	44-45
Off to Fish on a Bike	42
100th Year of Baseball	75
The Outing	59
Outside the Principal's Office	38
The Partygoers	30
The Peace Corps in Ethiopia	110-111
A Pilgrim's Progress	71
The Problem We All Live With	106-107
Rosie the Riveter	77
Santa on a Subway Train	76
Saying Grace	41
Shuffleton's Barber Shop	2
Solitaire	62
The Spirit of Education	91
The Swimming Hole	47
Tackled	26
The Tantrum	32
The Tatooist	46
Thanksgiving	78
Tiny Tim and Bob Cratchit	93
Traffic Conditions	61
Triple Self-Portrait	89
Walking to Church	84
The War Hero	82
The War Savings Bond	79
Willie Gillis in College	102
Willie Gillis on Leave	101
Willie Gillis at the USO	95
The Wonders of Radio	25
The Yarn Spinner	29

Picture Credits
Unless otherwise indicated, permission to reproduce all plates is by courtesy of the Estate of Norman Rockwell. The following pictures were provided by these agencies and institutions:
The Bettmann Archive: pages 1, 9(top), 11(bottom), 17(bottom)
The Boy Scouts of America: page 7(top right)
The New York Public Library: page 8(both)
The Norman Rockwell Museum at Stockbridge: pages 7(top left), 12(top, middle), 15, 17(top), 18(bottom), 19(bottom)
The Saturday Evening Post: pages 6-7(bottom), 9(bottom), 11(left)
UPI/Bettmann Newsphotos: pages 14(bottom), 16

Acknowledgments
The author and publisher would like to thank Janet Wu York, who edited and picture researched this book; and Mike Rose, who designed it. Special thanks to Thomas Rockwell, Estate of Norman Rockwell.